The Spiritual Life,

OR

Helps and Hindrances

BY

F. E. MARSH.

Wipf & Stock
PUBLISHERS
Eugene, Oregon

Wipf and Stock Publishers
199 W 8th Ave, Suite 3
Eugene, OR 97401

The Spiritual Life, or Helps and Hindrances
By Marsh, F.E.
ISBN: 1-59752-072-1
Publication date 1/26/2005
Previously published by Boone Publishing Company, 1958

Helps to the Spiritual Life.

CONTENTS.

		PAGE.
	INTRODUCTION: Phases of the Spiritual Life	5
Chapter 1.	PRAYER: The Secret of the Spiritual Life	13
,, 2.	SEPARATION: The Call of the Spiritual Life	24
,, 3.	THOROUGHNESS: The Meaning of the Spiritual Life	34
,, 4.	SCRIPTURE: The Feeder of the Spiritual Life	44
,, 5.	GOD: The Objective of the Spiritual Life	55
,, 6.	LOVE: The Heart of the Spiritual Life	69
,, 7.	HOLINESS: The Sanctity of the Spiritual Life	81
,, 8.	NEED: The Dependence of the Spiritual Life	98
,, 9.	DEPTH: The Inness of the Spiritual Life	112
,, 10.	THE HOLY SPIRIT: The Power of the Spiritual Life	127
,, 11.	THE SECOND BLESSING: or The Double of the Spiritual Life	142

INTRODUCTION.

Phases of the Spiritual Life.

An old man in the South of England often used a suggestive sentence in prayer. He would say, "Help us, O Lord, to deeper sink, that we may higher rise." Consciously or unconsciously he was indicating a deep spiritual axiom of the Christian life; for it is only as we get into the deeper things of the Spirit that we begin to rise into the heights of that life which is life indeed.

Every one knows the importance of a deep foundation to a high building. In looking at the Times Building in Broadway, New York, the first impression we get is, that this structure of over twenty stories would hardly stand the blast of some terrific cyclone, but when it is known there are some five or six stories beneath the surface as foundation, it is realised that its foundation is its stability and therefore its security. When God speaks of bringing His judgment upon Edom, He tells the inhabitants of Dedan to turn back and "dwell deep" (Jer. xlix. 8). Their separation from Edom and their dwelling in some secret place of safety would be their security. The same holds good in the Christian life. There is a needs be for clear and definite separation from everything that is not in the line of God's will, and to dwell in the secret place of the presence of the Most High. In the old days when there were constant feuds between the English and the Scots, those who lived on the borders of either country were in anything but a happy situation. Those too, who live as near as possible to the world, and yet hold on to Christ are in no happier position. There is a necessity not only to come out and be separate from the world, but also to come into the banqueting house of full fellowship with the Lord.

There were at least four circles of those who came in contact with Christ. There were the seventy disciples who were actively engaged in the Lord's work, in going at His bidding to preach to the lost sheep of the house of Israel, and who were eminently successful, for the devils were subject to them (Luke x. 17). There were the twelve who were chosen by Him, and who knew in some measure what it was to have fellowship with Him, for they are said to be "with Him." Then there were the three out of the twelve who were specially privileged to see the manifestation of His glory, and suffering, and power (Luke ix. 32; Matt. xxvi. 37; Mark v. 37); and, lastly, there was one who came nearer to Him than any other and entered into the secret purpose of His coming into the world, and that one was Mary of Bethany, for she anointed Him for His burial. These have their correspondence among the Lord's people to-day. There are those who have their names written in heaven and who are busily engaged in the Lord's work; there are those who know something of communion with the Lord in having left all and followed Him; there is yet another section who have a larger experience, in suffering with Christ, in seeing the manifestation of His power, and in beholding the shining forth of His personal glory; while there is yet another circle who, through sitting at the feet of Jesus, are quite enough for Him to make known to them His secret purposes.

Introduction. 7

Years ago, in the days of American slavery, there came to the lead mines on the Iowa side of the Mississippi river, a slave who had been entrusted by his master to make an effort to earn sufficient to free himself, his wife and children. After a little, he found a partner to work with him. They sunk a shaft to the average depth of eighty feet, but found no paying deposit of ore. This brought them to the end of their resources, and exhausted the partner's endurance. The slave was able to work at his shaft occasionally, while doing odd jobs for the other miners. For awhile he went on cheerfully, but hope at last began to grow dim in him. He therefore made up his mind to make one last effort, in drilling a hole as deep into the rock as he could, and as he was doing so the drill suddenly fell through. He then knew that his efforts were successful. It was not long before he had made an orifice through which he let himself down into the cavern, when to his unspeakable delight, upon striking a light, he was fairly dazzled by the brilliance of the crystalline ore around him, and was gladdened by the fact that he stood in the presence of the illuminated price that was to buy his freedom. When he had gained the value of his freedom, he was confronted by the fact that his wife and children were still in bondage. What should he do? There were two ways presented to him. He could either drift along the crevice at the same level of his first discovery, or he could go deeper down for a second store of mineral wealth. The old miners advised him to follow the former course, but his own heart seemed to say, "Go down." And down he began to drill again. His own intuition was soon rewarded, for he struck another opening much larger and richer than the first. This time his hopes were abundantly surpassed, and it was not long before his wife and children were emancipated, a good house erected and furnished, and a large farm purchased and stocked, besides which he had an ample capital left over for business transactions.

This incident is a parable. All believers know what it is to receive the Redeemer, Who has procured redemption for them by His atoning death, which redemption means freedom from condemnation and deliverance from sin's power; but too many are content to follow the "drift" of a negative salvation, instead of going into the deeper experience of a positive salvation, in possessing the fulness of the Spirit's power, for their own sufficient equipment and in blessing to others. It is well that we should with Jacob see the way cast up to heaven in the mediatorial work of Christ, and the angels of blessing coming to us in consequence; but it is better to be conquered by the Lord at Peniel, for it is there that the joint of self is displaced and power is obtained through faith's clinging. It is well to be protected from judgment in the Egypt of the world's condemnation, by the blood of the Paschal Lamb; but it is better to come out of Egypt and to be delivered from our enemies by means of the Red Sea of the Lord's delivering grace; and better still to be led through the wilderness of sin into the Land of Promise, for God deals with us according to the riches of His grace, in giving us every spiritual blessing in Christ.

Every careful reader of the New Testament must see that in the Godhead there is a trinity of blessing, no matter what note we strike on the piano of truth.

There is *life from Christ* (John v. 25) which, like Ezekiel's river, makes us glad and healthy and fruitful as it touches us (Ezek. xlvii. 9-12); there is *life in Christ* (Rom. viii. 2), which means participation in all His fulness and unlimited riches, even as Ruth was made to participate in all the wealth of Boaz in her union with him; and there is *life with Christ*, which means fellowship with Him, or having everything in common with Him, as Elijah and Elisha had when they went together from Bethel to Jordan (II. Kings ii. 2).

When we come to the Shiloh waters of God's peace we find there are three streams which flow one into the other. *Peace with God* is the first stream which flows, like the living water of Ezekiel from beside the altar of sacrifice (Ezek. xlvii. 1). *The peace of God* is the garrison to keep the citadel of our heart from care and worry, as we are careful for nothing, prayerful in everything, and thankful for anything (Phil. iv. 6, 7); and the *God of peace* enshrines Himself in the sanctuary of our being to keep us absolutely and wholly for Himself. Thus we have not only the blessing but the Blesser.

It is not without significance that the apostle replied to the jailor's question, " What must I do to be saved ?" " Believe on the Lord Jesus Christ." That is, I take it, to believe in Him as Lord, Jesus, Christ. To believe in Him *as Jesus* means to be saved by Him. To believe in Him *as Christ* means to be sanctified in Him; and to believe in Him *as Lord* signifies, He is sovereign over us. The practical question now comes, do we know the Lord and His blessings in the larger and deeper sense of the word? No one who comes in contact with the Christians of our day can help being convinced that there are those who are, like Peter, following their Lord afar off; that there are those who are like the Ephesian Christians, who do not know the Spirit's filling; that there are those, like the Thessalonians, who have a defective faith; that there are those who, like Ananias, are keeping back part of the price; that there are those like the unspiritual and factious Corinthians, who are "carnal"; that there are those who are in bondage, like the legal Galatians; that there are those who have left their first love, like the Church at Laodicea; and that there are those who are tolerant to error, like the Church at Pergamos. Mr. Moody was not far wrong when, in calling together a conference at Northfield some few years ago, said, "There are in the churches stores of unconsecrated wealth, unused or misused talents, multitudes at ease in Zion, witnesses who bear no testimony for their Lord, workers without the Spirit's conquering power, teachers who speak without authority, disciples who follow afar off, forms without life, Church machinery substituted for inward life and power."

The question may be asked, "How are we to be the opposite to what the great evangelist said too many Christians were?" There is one answer, namely, obedience to the Lord.

When Arthur of Round Table fame lay a-dying, he commissioned Bedivere to take his beautiful sword and throw it into the lake. He said,

"take Excalibur,
And fling him far into the middle mere:
Watch what thou seest, and lightly bring me word."

The knight hesitated to do his master's bidding, but at last at his lord's repeated command he made his way, sword in hand, to the margin of the lake. Ere he obeyed Arthur's word he looked at the hilt of the sword as it flashed in the moonlight, and saw that it

> "twinkled with diamond studs,
> Myriads of topaz-lights, and jacinth-work
> Of subtlest jewelry."

He was so dazzled by the beauty of the sword that he went and hid it among the waterflags, and then went back to wounded Arthur, who looked up to him and said,

> "Hast thou performed the mission which I gave?
> What is it thou hast seen, or what hast heard?"

He knew by the answer that Bedivere gave that he had not obeyed his directions. The king tells him so, and charges him with his unfaithfulness, and bids him go the second time and do his will. As he goes he argues with himself against the king's command, and again failed to do as he was bid, and gave the same reply to Arthur upon his return. Whereupon the king with scathing word said,

> "Ah, miserable and unkind, untrue,
> Unknightly, traitor-hearted! Woe is me!
> Authority forgets a dying king,
> Laid widow'd of the power in his eye
> That bows the will. I see thee what thou art,
> For thou, the latest-left of all my knights,
> In whom should meet the offices of all,
> Thou wouldst betray me for the precious hilt;
> Either from lust of gold, or like a girl
> Valuing the giddy pleasure of the eyes.
> Yet, for a man may fail in duty twice,
> And the third time may prosper, get thee hence:
> But, if thou spare to fling Excalibur,
> I will arise and slay thee with my hands."

Stung to the quick he rushes down to the water-side and, without look or hesitation, he grasps the sword and flings it far into the mere. As Excalibur, flung through the air, nears the surface of the lake, there

> "rose an arm
> Clothed in white samite, mystic, wonderful,
> And caught him by the hilt, and brandish'd him
> Three times, and drew him under in the mere."

Bedivere had no vision till he had obeyed, and obeyed fully, King Arthur's will. The same is true of the believer in Christ. The Lord as the Almighty will not walk in us till we fully come out from the world to Himself (II. Cor. vi. 14-18); He will not give the Spirit's fulness of power unless we obey Him (Acts v. 32); He will only direct our steps as we acknowledge Him in all our ways (Prov. iii. 6); and He will only give us "open vision" as we are right with Him.

Helps to the Spiritual Life.

CHAPTER I.

PRAYER: THE SECRET OF THE SPIRITUAL LIFE.

"Tell me, what is the secret of your success?" was the question put to Evan Roberts, when referring to the Welsh Revival. "There is no secret," was his reply. "All that is needed is reliance on the great promise, 'Ask and ye shall receive.'" Prayer is the secret of the deeper life. Prayer is a *sin-killer*. No one can sin and pray, for prayer will either make us cease from sin, or sin will make us cease from prayer. Prayer is a *power-bringer*. It is the hand which touches the hem of the garment of Divine grace, and causes the life which is in the Divine One to flow into us. Prayer is a *victory-giver*. Bunyan's Christian found that the weapon of "all-prayer" was sufficient to wound and defeat the adversary, who would stop him in his progress as a pilgrim. Prayer is a *holiness-promoter*. It is like the gentle dew which falls upon the thirsty plants, and causes them to be refreshed and to fructify. Prayer is a *dispute-adjuster*. Let any two brethren who are at loggerheads get on their knees, and ask the Lord about any disputed matter, and they will find the Lord saying to their troubled spirits, "Peace, be still." Prayer is an *obstacle-remover*, as Peter found when an angel came in answer to the prayers of the saints, and delivered him from the prison of Herod's hate; and prayer is a *Christ-revealer*, for it clarifies our vision, and enables us to see the unseen.

We cannot do without prayer. The spiritual life is born in prayer, and it flourishes, and is strong, as it lives in that same atmosphere.

> " Why, therefore, should we do ourselves this wrong,
> Or others—that we are not always strong ;
> That we are ever overborne with care ;
> That we should ever weak or heartless be,
> Anxious or troubled, when with us is prayer,
> And joy, and strength, and courage are with Thee ?"

There are seven strands in the cable of prayer, and these are denominated in the seven words which are associated with the inner life of prayer, as revealed in the New Testament.

I. THE ART OF PRAYER IS THE PRAYER FROM THE HEART. Of Elijah we read, " He prayed earnestly," or as it might be read, " with prayer he prayed." His prayer was no cold and formal petition, but it was all aglow with intense and deliberate asking. He illustrates, in a striking manner, two of the essential requisites in prayer, namely, *heart* and *art*. When the warm heart of earnest feeling and the holy art of definite pleading are present, there is sure to be effectual prayer.

Longfellow says,

> " The heart giveth grace unto every art."

George Macdonald says something similar,

> " Better to have the poet's heart than brain,
> Feeling than song ; but better far than both,
> To be a song, a music of God's making."

When the music of the Spirit's pleading is making our petition, there is sure to be the warm heart of felt need, and this at once will lead us to the art of pointed petition. The thing which made Elijah to pray as he did, was the man that he was. When our Great High Priest comes with the lighted torch of His grace, and ignites the wood of our being into a holy flame, then the sweet-smelling savours of our definite requests ascend acceptably to God, and bring down the benediction of His love.

We recognise that the art of prayer is a sense of desperate need, for as an old writer has said:

"It is not the arithmetic of our prayers, how many they are; nor the rhetoric of our prayers, how eloquent they be; nor the geometry of our prayers, how long they be; nor the music of our prayers, how sweet our voice may be; nor the logic of our prayers, how argumentative they may be; nor the method of our prayers, how orderly they may be; nor even the theology of our prayers, how good the doctrine may be—which God cares for. Fervency of spirit is that which availeth much."

II. THE SENSE OF NEED WILL MAKE US SENSIBLE TO THE NECESSITY OF PRAYER. The Holy Spirit, like a skilled artist in painting a picture, has given to us in the words which are rendered prayer, suggestive touches as to the qualifications which go to make up its volume.

We are told, "the effectual *prayer* of a righteous man availeth much" (Jas. v. 16). The word "*prayer*" in this instance signifies *a sense of deed*. [The substantive "*deesis*" occurs nineteen times, and the verb "*deomai*" occurs twenty-three times, and in every case more or less there is a sense of need expressed in the use of the words.] The noun is rendered "*supplication*" in Acts

i. 14, where we are told the disciples met " with one accord in prayer and *supplication*." They were conscious of their deep need of the Spirit's equipment for life and service; hence, they were pleading in prayer and supplication for this enduement. The verb is rendered "*besought*" in Luke v. 12, and "*making request*" in Romans i. 10. In the former passage we have described to us a man full of leprosy, who fell on his face before Christ and besought Him to cleanse him; and in the latter passage the apostle is praying that he might have a prosperous journey to the saints in Rome. In each case there is a sense of need, and an earnest desire to have that need met. We pray so little because we feel so little. If we only realised it, there are always four petitions which we could make to the Lord, as Southey says,

> " Four things which are not in Thy Treasury,
> I lay before thee, Lord, with this petition :
> My nothingness, my wants,
> My sins, and my contrition."

The sense of our sin will make us cry out with Isaiah, " Woe is me," till we know the cleansing of the Lord's sacrifice, which removes sin from us, and fits us for future service. The consciousness of our nothingness, as we are confronted with the demoniacs of evil, will make us cry out with the Syrophenician woman, " Lord, help me "; and the wants which press us on every side, and the meagre supply we have to meet them, will make us say with Andrew, as he contemplated the few loaves and fishes and compared them with the needy multitude around him, " What are these among so many ?"

III. THE HEART'S DESIRE VOICES ITS REQUEST IN THE INTENSITY OF ITS LONGING. "All things, whatsoever ye shall ask in prayer, believing ye shall receive." The word "*ask*," in Matt. xxi. 22, is rendered "*desire*" in Mark xi. 24, "*begged*" in Matt. xxvii. 58, "*petitions*" in 1. John v. 15, and "*requests*" in Phil. iv. 6. The Greek word and its cognate are found altogether in some seventy-four passages, and their usage suggests *the thought of need expressed in definite request*, and there is also the further suggestion of the difference between the suppliant who asks a favour and the one who grants it. Unless the heart of desire moves the lips of petition, we pray to no purpose. On the other hand, the inward desire without petition is sometimes the most potent in its pleading.

> "Prayer is the soul's sincere desire,
> Uttered or unexpressed,
> The motion of a hidden fire
> That trembles in the breast."

When Hannah was praying in the temple, we read that she spake in her heart, only her lips moved but her voice was not heard. Eli thought she was under the influence of drink, and rebuked her accordingly; whereupon she replied, "I have drunk neither wine nor strong drink, but have poured out my soul before the Lord." When Eli heard this he said to her, "Go in peace and the God of Israel grant thee thy petition that thou hast asked of Him" (1. Sam. i. 9-17). Her moving lips were thought to be the mutterings of a daughter of Belial, as Eli judged, but he did not see the moved heart of earnest prayer beneath the surface. As a man thinketh in his heart, so is he, and as a man prayeth in his heart, so God estimates the real worth of the prayer.

IV. THE CONSECRATED PETITIONER PRAYS A PETITION WHICH EVIDENCES HIS CONSECRATION. *The consecration of prayer* is suggested by two Greek words ("*proseuche*" and "*proseuchomai*") which occur 125 times. These words indicate *the condition of the one who prays*. They convey more than mere asking; they suggest that the one who prays is *right with the Lord. They are restricted to prayer to God*. Sometimes they suggest the place of prayer (Luke xix. 46), as being a place set apart for that purpose. The first word is a compound word, one part meaning a vow and the other signifying a turning towards; therefore it is an attitude of worship as expressed by prayer.

When we remember there can be no worship without being in communion with the Lord, we can see that consecration is an essential element in effectual prayer. Take but three instances where the word occurs. Of Christ it is said, "As He *prayed*," He was transfigured (Luke ix. 29). The glory of the Christ was latent in Him before He prayed, but the praying caused the glory to become patent. The church of Antioch were able to send forth Paul and Barnabas on their great missionary journey because they had "fasted and *prayed*." The church could act in a right way towards them because they were right with the Lord (Acts xiii. 1-3). It is not any one that will do to pray over the sick; hence the elders of the church are named as those who pray over the sick one (Jas. v. 14), which presupposes that the elders are not only men of experience in the things of the Lord, but those who are in close touch with Him. Hence "the prayer of faith saves the sick." This implies that there is the faithfulness of a consistent life; for no one ever yet prayed the prayer of faith who had not behind it the life of faithfulness.

Burns, in his Cotter's Saturday night, says,

> "They never sought in vain,
> That sought the Lord aright."

To be right with the Lord, is sure to secure blessing from the Lord.

V. THE HELP OF PRAYER IS EXPRESSED IN THE HELP WHICH COMES IN RESPONSE TO ITS CRY. The man out of whom Christ cast the legion of demons "*prayed* that he might be with Him" (Mark v. 18). The Greek word rendered "*prayed*" in the above passage means *to call beside one*, that something may be done, or said. It is rendered "*besought*" three times, in Luke viii. 31, 32, 41. The demons prayed that Christ would not allow them to go into the "abyss" (R.V.), but suffer them to go into the herd of swine; and Jairus pleaded with Christ to go with Him to heal his daughter. Paul uses the word in indicating that the aim of true ministry is to "*beseech*" (R.V., "intreating by us") men to be reconciled to God (II. Cor. v. 20); and the same word is given in II. Cor. i. 4, "*comforteth*," when Paul speaks of the comfort which the Lord gives to His own afflicted ones.

Here is a great fact, no one ever called to Christ to come near to assist but that He responded. The centurion was found at His feet "*beseeching* Him" (Matt. viii. 5) to heal his servant, and at once Christ said, "I will come and heal him." The multitude "*besought*" Him that they might touch Him to their healing, and as many as touched Him were healed (Mark vi. 56). The leper came "beseeching Him" for cleansing, and at once He said, " I will ; be thou clean " (Mark i. 40). The friends of the deaf man "*beseech* Him" to cure him, and immediately He says to the deaf ears, " Be opened " (Mark vii. 32). The blind man is brought to Him, and they "*besought* Him" to touch him, which He did to the restoration of his sight. We have to do with the same Christ, and whether for ourselves, or others, we may be sure He will come near and do as we wish.

> " More things are wrought by prayer
>   Than this world dreams of. Wherefore, let thy voice
>   Rise like a fountain for me night and day.
>   For what are men better than sheep and goats
>   That nourish a blind life within the brain,
>   If, knowing God, they lift not hands of prayer
>   Both for themselves and those who call them friend ?
>   For so the whole world round is every way
>   Bound by gold chains about the feet of God."

We may find others about " the feet of God." Let us therefore prize this ministry, and exercise it continually, for there is no service valued so much in heaven as this, nor any other which brings such benefit to men and help to the suppliant.

VI. THE CONFIDENCE OF PRAYER IS OBTAINED BY THE RECOGNITION OF PROMISE. Christ says, " In that day ye shall *ask* me nothing " (John xvi. 23). The questionings would all be answered in the fuller revelation of the Holy Spirit. Christ uses the word in relation to His disciples, in referring to His ministry on their behalf in the frequent formula, "I *pray*" (John xiv. 16; xvi. 26; xvii. 9, 15, 20). The word "*erotao*" signifies *to enquire, implying familiarity*, being on an equality with one. He was, and He is, continually enquiring of the Father, what is His will in relation to us. The Apostle John uses the word in 1. John v. 16, about the sin unto death: "I do not say he shall *pray* for it," that is, enquire about it. All sin is unto death, but here is a sin which tends directly to death. In the previous sentence we are told there is a sin not unto death, for which we may "ask," and that the prayer is answered. Why should not the prayer be answered in each case? The explanation is found in the words used. In the first instance the word used ("*aiteo*") implies the humble petition of an inferior; but the second word ("*erotao*") means to make request as an equal, therefore it is used in an authoritative sense. As Canon Fausett says, "to request for a sin unto death (*intercede authoritatively for it*, as though we were more merciful than God) savours of presumption; prescribing to God what lies out of the bounds of brotherly yearning (because one sinning unto death is thereby demonstrated not to be truly a brother), how shall He inflict and withhold His righteous judgments. Jesus Himself intercedes, not for the world which hardens itself in unbelief, but for those given to Him out of it." We may humbly intercede for the one who is sinning, but we have not a right to authoritatively ask on uncertain ground. There are times when we may authoritatively make request, that is, to humbly require God to do certain things, provided our authority is based on the authority of God's promise.

VII. THE INTERCESSION OF PRAYER IS THE HIGHEST FORM OF MINISTRY. This thought is embodied in the word " *enteuxis*," which only occurs twice (1. Tim. ii. 1 ; iv. 5). The thought associated with it is, not only *interceding for others*, but a falling in with another to talk over matters, and for each to ask something from the other, thus to have *fellowship*.

Combining the two thoughts, do we not get the principle, that he who would plead successfully for others, must be in the place of fellowship with the Lord. If we have the ear of God's attention, through our whole-hearted communion with Himself, we may be sure of the hand of His aid.

George Muller, in his ninety-third year, said, that " every stone in the Homes at Ashley Down was the result of prayer." The same is true in the spiritual life of our character, every grace is the result of prayer, not as the ground of bestowment, but as the secret of obtainment. Our power for others comes from the same source. Rabbi Duncan, the famous professor of Hebrew, confesses that the one thing that won him to Christ was the prayers of Dr. Mearns. It was no logical argument that turned him from atheism, but the influence of a true and reverent believer's prayer, conveying the sense of a living fellowship between him and the object of his worship.

> " To talk with God—no breath is lost ;
>   Talk on, talk on !
> To walk with God—no strength is lost ;
>   Walk on, walk on !
> To wait on God—no time is lost ;
>   Wait on, wait on !

To grind the axe—no work is lost;
      Grind on, grind on !
The work is quicker, better done,
Not needing half the strength laid on ;
      Grind on.
Martha stood—but Mary sat ;
Martha murmured much at that ;
Martha cared—but Mary heard
Listening to the Master's word,
And the Lord her choice preferr'd,
      Sit on—hear on.
Work without God is labour lost ;
      Work on, work on !
Full soon you'll learn it to your cost ;
      Toil on, toil on !
Little is much, when God is in it ;
Man's busiest day's not worth God's minute ;
Much is little everywhere,
If God the labour do not share ;
So work with God, and nothing's lost,
Who works with Him, does best and most,
      Work on, work on !"

CHAPTER II.

SEPARATION: THE CALL OF THE SPIRITUAL LIFE.

Dr. Harry Guinness relates an incident in the life of the Missionary Institute which used to be under his charge at Curbar. On one occasion there was an insufficient supply of water, and it could not be accounted for, as it was known that there was an abundant supply at the source. At last they came to the conclusion there was something wrong with the channels, and the conclusion proved to be correct, for a frog was found in the pipe. It was a mystery how he got there, whether he had got into the pipe when a tadpole and had grown till he was a frog, or had squeezed himself in, could not be determined, but there he was, and stopping the way. The above is an illustration of what often occurs in the lives of God's people.

The statements of God's Word confirm the fact, that there are abundant supplies in the resources of His grace to meet the need of the believer. The mercy which sought and found us is abundant in the bestowment of its blessings (1. Pet. i. 3); as the prodigal found when he came back to his father's heart and hearth. The *grace* which saves, secures and sanctifies, is abounding in the fulness of its resource (Rom. v. 20), even as the waters of the flood covered every high mountain. The *life* which quickens from the death of sin, is not only that which makes us one with Christ, but it is an abundant life to make us fruitful in all the graces of the Spirit (John

x. 10), even as Ezekiel's river brings life and fruitfulness wherever it flows. The *peace* which calms amid every trial, and stills in every tempest of temptation, is unceasing and effective in its ministry (Psa. lxxii. 7), even as Christ said to the tempest-tossed lake, " Peace, be still," and there was a great calm. The *joy* which is unspeakable in its nature, and independent of circumstances, is one which is described as being " abundant in Christ Jesus " (Phil. i. 26), even as the inhabitants of Samaria found through the ministry of Philip the Evangelist. The *goodness* of the promises of God's house, and the cheer of His presence, are satisfying to those who are found abiding in Christ, for like the Psalmist they are " abundantly satisfied " (Psa. xxxvi. 8), even as the five thousand found more than enough, when Christ fed them, and the promise of the Lord in answer to our prayer, as His power works unhindered in us, is that He will " do exceeding abundantly above all we ask or think " (Eph. iii. 20), even as Ruth found when Boaz, the mighty man of wealth, not only supplied all her need, but made her to share all his riches.

As we stand before the assurances of God's unlimited supply, *are we not conscious that we do not know a tithe of these things in our own personal experiences?* It seems to me there are *three great hindrances* which back the inflow of God's power in our hearts to our joy, and the outflow of that same power to others' blessing: and these are *worldliness, selfishness* and *prayerlessness*. These three hindrances lead our thoughts in three different directions: *outward*, there is the hurtful bane of worldliness; *inward*, there is the possibility of the blight of selfishness; and *Godward*, there may be the curse of prayerlessness, which bolts up the doors of heaven. Let us look at these three hindrances.

I. SEPARATION FROM THE WORLD.

In the long line of the Doges, in the grand palace in Venice, one space is empty, and the black curtain which covers it attracts more attention than any one of the fine portraits of the merchant kings. From that panel, now so unsightly, once smiled the sallow face of Marino Falieri, afterwards found guilty of treason against the State, and blotted out, so far as might be, from remembrance. In the portrait gallery, which we find in the epistles of Paul, there is something which is very like what is said of Marino Falieri. *Demas* was one who was honoured in sending friendly salutation with the Apostle Paul to the church at Colosse and to Philemon (Col. iv. 14; Philemon 24); and yet of him the apostle had to say sadly, in the after days, in writing to Timothy: " Demas hath forsaken me, having loved this present world " (II. Tim. iv. 10). No sadder statement could be made of any one; yet, alas ! too often it has to be said, and more often it would be said, if the truth were known, that those who profess to love the Saviour, love this present world.

Let us briefly note *some of the things which God says about the world;* for if we know the Lord's mind about it, we must surely avoid those things of which He says, " Be separate."

Worldliness is evil in its nature. The world is described as this " present evil world " (Gal. i. 4), and we are told that its evil is a trinity, namely, " the lust of the flesh, the lust of the eyes, and the pride of life "

(1. John ii. 16). It was the lust of the flesh which tripped up Balaam to his destruction. It was the lust of the eyes which led Achan astray, when he saw and took the Babylonish garment and the gold, and thus he came under the swift judgment of God. It was the pride of life which filled the heart of Haman with avarice and ambition, and which caused him to be hanged upon the gallows he had erected for Mordecai. Generally speaking, worldliness is anything which takes our heart away from God, and erects therein anything or anyone in the place of Christ.

Worldliness is downward in its tendency. We read of " the course of this world " (Eph. ii. 2). That " course " is away from God, for it is " according to the prince of the power of the air." " When Henry IV. of France asked the Duke of Alva's opinion respecting some of the astronomical mysteries of heaven, he said, ' Sire, I have so much to do on earth, that I have no leisure to think of heaven.' " How many there are who might say the same thing, if they would but give a true statement as to the tendency of their lives; yea, even some of God's professing children are so occupied all the week with the muck-rake of their own concerns, that they have no time to think of the heavenly things above them.

Worldliness is contaminating in its influence. One of the essentials which describes those who know pure religion, is to keep " unspotted from the world " (Jas. i. 27). The word " *unspotted* " occurs in only four places in the New Testament. In three instances it is rendered " *without spot.*" Once it is used in connection with Christ, in describing the perfection of His nature. He is said to be without blemish and " *without spot* "

(I. Pet. i. 19). Paul charged Timothy to keep " the commandment" which he had laid upon him in faithfully discharging his duty "*without spot*" (I. Tim. vi. 14); and believers generally in view of the Lord's return are to be " found of Him in peace *without spot* and blameless" (II. Pet. iii. 14); and we are also to keep ourselves "*unspotted* from the world." Mr. Spurgeon said : " The bloom of the hawthorn looks like snow in Richmond Park, but nearer London, or by the roadsides, its virgin whiteness is sadly stained. Contact with the world has just such an effect upon our piety : we must away to the far-off Paradise to see its unsullied purity, and we must be much alone with God, if we would maintain a gracious life below."

Worldliness is antagonistic to God. " The friendship of the world is enmity with God " (James iv. 4). There is a suggestive contrast found in the epistle by James. We read that " he who would be a friend of the world is an enemy of God," while our attention is also called to one who was " a friend of God " and therefore an enemy to the world (Jas. ii. 23). Abraham is repeatedly called " the friend of God " (II. Chron. xx. 7 ; Isa. xli. 8). Although we are not distinctly told when God specifically called Him His friend, yet there are indications when He did so. It was after Abraham had refused to receive from the King of Sodom the gifts by which he would enrich him, that the Lord came to His servant and said, " I am thy Shield and thy Exceeding Great Reward " (Gen. xiv. 1 ; xv. 1). The King of Sodom is typical of the world, and as Abraham would not associate with him, nor receive anything from him, so the believer should keep from the world which would enrich him at the expense of principle, and lead to the denial of Christ.

Worldliness is corrupting in its association. We read of the " corruption that is in the world " (II. Pet. i. 4), and also of " the pollutions of the world " (II. Pet. ii. 20). "*Corruption*" signifies the putrefaction of a dead body, and "*pollution*" comes from a word meaning to stain. The world leaves its mark upon those who associate with it, and infects with its corrupting influence. Association with it always leads to disassociation from the Lord. There is no greater proof of this than when the child of God neglects prayer and the meditation on God's Word. All the while Abraham was in Egypt he had no communication from the Lord, and it was not till he came back to Bethel that he knew the Lord's restoring grace and had communion again with Him.

Worldliness is unsatisfying in its pleasures. "The fashion of this world passeth away" (I. Cor. vii. 31 ; I. John ii. 17). The image which the apostle employs is taken from *a shifting scene on a stage*. The pleasures last but for a season. How true are the words of Thomas Moore :

> " This world is all a fleeting show,
>   For man's illusion given ;
> The smiles of joy, the tears of woe,
> Deceitful shine, deceitful flow—
> There's nothing true, but Heaven !"

The world is hateful in its opposition. This is especially true if the child of God is thorough in his devotion to Christ, is separate from all that is evil, and bears a pointed testimony against the hollowness and the unsatisfying nature of the things of the world. The

Christian should never expect any consideration from the world, and more, he should never be prepared to receive any, for the world knoweth us not, and the Lord tells us not to marvel if we are hated by it (1. John iii. 1, 13).

> "The world's all title-page; there's no contents;
> The world's all face; the man who shows his heart,
> Is hooted for his nudities, and scorn'd."

There are many things which are perfectly harmless in themselves, but which become hurtful because of their associations. It may be asked, "What *general rule* would you lay down for our guidance as to our attitude to the world? Separation from it is the Lord's direction, clear and definite; and as we come out from it in obedience to Him we find ourselves not only in the place of safety, but in the position of power. To be specific, the following *seven rules* should be followed :—

1. Go to no place where the Lord will not take you.

2. Be found in no company which is not helpful to your Christian life.

3. Have no pleasure except in the company of those who are the Lord's.

4. Be no party to any transaction upon which you cannot seek your Lord's approval.

5. Listen to no voice which would lead you away from the truth of God's Word.

6. Allow no pleasure to interfere with your attendance at the means of grace.

7. Whatsoever you do, do all to the glory of God.

II. SEPARATION FROM SELFISHNESS.

The general principle upon which self acts is, Get all you can : give as little as you can : and keep as much as you can for yourself. It thoroughly believes in the words of Shakespeare—

> " I to myself am dearer than a friend ";

and,
> " What need we any spur, but our own cause,
> To prick us to redress " ?

But such suggested courses should not characterise the child of God, for the principle of the Gospel is against it. For those who have come to Christ, He says, " If any man will come after Me, let him deny himself." This is *more than mere self-denial* so called, which means the denial of certain things to self. Christ's words mean *the denial of self itself.* This is not according to nature, but it certainly is according to grace, and can only be known as we experimentally enter into the fact, that self is crucified with Christ.

Some one has said, everybody has *four selves :* First, the self which everybody knows ; second, the self which our near friends know ; third, the self which we ourselves know ; fourth, the self which only God knows." However much we may differentiate self, it is self in whatever relation it is found, and it ever aims at its own aggrandisement and benefit. Sin is the soil in which it grows, covetousness is the spring which causes it to act, and gain is that at which it aims.

One has said, " The essence of all immorality and sin, is the making self the centre from which we subordinate all other things and interests." On the other hand, when Christ is the Centre everything is subordinate to Him.

Oh, horrid self, in how many ways it seeks to show itself! It is a very chameleon in its changefulness. There is a *humble self*, which is very proud of its humility and, like Agag before Samuel, can fawn itself to the ground; there is a *hypocritical self* which can feign one thing and be another, like Jacob before Isaac, when he robbed his brother of his blessing; there is a *covetous self*, which cares not who sinks so long as it can swim, and grabs at all it can, like Judas with the money in the bag; there is an *ambitious self*, which can never be satisfied but by being at the top, like the Pharisees, who loved the uppermost seats; there is a *conceited self*, which suffers with a big head and an inflated heart, and is conspicuous by the use of the personal pronoun I, like the Pharisee praying in the temple; there is an *earnest self*, which will go out of its way to carry out its designs, like Saul of Tarsus, and which prides itself on being zealous in the cause of God; and there is a *religious self*, which always thinks itself holier than others, and which is ready to go to any expense in the prosecution of its own ideas, like Micah in the Book of Judges.

III. SEPARATION FROM PRAYERLESSNESS.

More things are lost for want of prayer than the Christian dreams of. Prayer is the key which opens the door of God's provision, therefore to want it is to be destitute of what the Lord has to give. Prayer is the atmosphere which eradiates the rays of God's love, therefore to be without is to be cold and indifferent. Prayer is the mystic wand which silvers the dark caverns of life and makes everything bright with the brightness of God's care; therefore to be without it means to be in the darkness of complaining, and in the poverty which a murmuring spirit always brings. Prayer is the switch-board which the hand of faith uses to turn on the electric current of God's energising power; therefore to be without it is to be like Samson, shorn of his strength, and to be in the helplessness of self-effort and in the prison house of despair. Prayer is the feeder of courage, which makes us aim at the impossible and to achieve it, even as the Japanese soldier, fired by the spirit of patriotism, is regardless of consequences; therefore to be without it shows we are hiding ourselves in the den of cowardice and are guilty of faithlessness to the Lord. Prayer is the soil in which the graces of the Spirit grow to perfection and which causes them to blossom and fructify to the benefit of others; therefore not to be planted therein is to be barren of the Spirit's fruit. And prayer is the telescope which enables us to look into the heaven of God's secrets; therefore to lack it is to be in the darkness.

Whatever hindrance it is that is keeping back the fulness of the Lord's blessing and hindering our entering into the deeper things of His grace, let Him come, with the kindly whip of His discipline and the expulsive power of His action, and turn everything out of the temple of our being which He has bought with His blood and consecrated to Himself, that in the days to come every whit may utter His glory.

CHAPTER III.

THOROUGHNESS: THE MEANING OF THE SPIRITUAL LIFE.

Among the many saints who have been noted for their thoroughness in the service of God was Nehemiah. He was thorough in everything he undertook. There were no half measures with him. He was all aglow, and always on the go. Difficulties did not daunt him, nor opposition haunt him. He seems to say without saying it:

> "Let come what will, I mean to bear it out,
> And either live with glorious victory
> Or die with fame, renown'd in chivalry.
> He is not worthy of the honeycomb
> That shuns the hive because the bees have stings."

He would have no half-heartedness, nor would he allow any compromise for one moment. He was angry when he saw some of the Jews had taken usury from their brethren, and insisted upon them restoring what they had taken (Neh. v. 1-13). He would not tolerate the alliance of Eliashib the priest with Tobiah, and his making him comfortable in the house of the Lord. He therefore cast forth all the household stuff of Tobiah out of the chamber (Neh. xiii. 4-9). He rebuked the people for their selfishness in not supporting the Levites in the work of the Lord (Neh. xiii. 10). He raised the ringing voice of his testimony against the Sabbath breakers, and with the strong hand of determination he shut the gates of Jerusalem in the faces of those who would sell their merchandise on the Sabbath, so that they found themselves outside of the city, and he also threatened that he would lay hands on any who would further desecrate the Lord's day (Neh. xiii. 15-21). He reviled those who had contaminated themselves and disobeyed the Lord by taking wives from the heathen, and reminded them how Solomon had been led astray by " outlandish women " (Neh. xiii. 26). He prayed against those who had defiled the holy garments of the priesthood ; and with swift feet chased one of the relatives of Eliashib, who was son-in-law to San-Ballat the Horonite, and was not satisfied till he could ring out a clear note of testimony, saying : " Thus cleansed I them from all strangers, and appointed the words of the priests and the Levites, everyone in his business " (Neh. xiii. 28-30). The same must hold in relation to the child of God. The hesitancy of half-heartedness, the vacillation of compromise, the unequal yoke of an unholy alliance, the nauseousness of lukewarmness, are things which God will not tolerate.

I. THE " THROUGHLY " OF CLEANSING.

There are two " *throughlys* " in the New Testament which bring this out. They indicate the negative and the positive sides of sanctification. John the Baptist proclaimed that he would " *throughly* purge His floor " (Matt. iii. 12). The Greek word rendered " *throughly purge,*" signifies to " *cleanse through.*" It is made up of two words, " *katharizo,*" which means to cleanse, and " *dia,*" which means through. The leper used the word " *katharizo* " when he said, " If Thou wilt Thou canst make me *clean* " ; and Christ responded, " I will, be thou *clean*," and immediately his leprosy was "*cleansed*" (Matt. viii. 2-3). "*Dia*" is used in Luke xvii. 11, where we are told that Christ passed "*through*" the midst of Samaria and Galilee on the way to Jerusalem. Thus we see that this compound word signifies to cleanse all through; even as a defiled pipe will be cleansed by the cleansing power of the water which flows through it. Rotherham renders the passage, " He will clear out His threshing-floor." Christ always cleans out before He comes in. He fits before He furnishes. He empties before He fills. He cleanses before He conforms. He purifies before He possesses. This is always God's order, as may be seen in the following Scriptures, where the thought of cleansing precedes the subsequent blessing mentioned.

The guilty conscience is purged by the atoning blood of Christ from the penalty and pollution of sin, that we may serve the Lord as His priests in priestly service, that is, as holy priests to offer up the spiritual sacrifices of a humble heart, of a whole-hearted consecration and in doing good to others (Heb. ix. 14; xiii. 15, 16).

The grand purpose that Christ had in loving the Church and giving Himself up in His infinite grace to death, was that He might sanctify and cleanse, and then present it to Himself as a bride prepared for her nuptial day (Eph. v. 26, 27).

The Lord hath stretched out the hand of His grace and saved us, in order to purify unto Himself a people, that He might then claim them as His own sacred possession in which the glory of His presence is to be enshrined (Titus ii. 14, R.V.).

The "*therefore*" of II. Cor. vii. 1, which gives the Divine reason why we are to cleanse ourselves from all filthiness of the flesh and of the spirit, is the prelude to knowing the Lord as the Almighty One, Who is to walk in us, that we may walk in all the precepts of His word in power (II. Cor. vi. 18, etc.).

Purity of heart is essential before we can see God. The vision of God is only given to those who look out from the cleansed windows of the redeemed soul (Matt. v. 8). As Esther purified and perfumed herself before she went into the presence of the King, so we are exhorted to be cleansed with pure water, that is, our hearts sprinkled from an evil conscience before we enter the presence of the Lord as His worshippers (Heb. x. 22). There can be no worship of the Lord unless we are right with Him.

The secret of prevailing prayer is to "call on the Lord out of a pure heart" (II. Tim. ii. 22). We cannot pray well if we walk ill. Holy hands in prayer hold the Lord to their power, and He holds them for His use.

Of the Lamb's wife it is said, ere she sat down to the marriage, "she hath made herself ready, being clothed in fine linen clean and white" (Rev. xix. 7-8). The feasting with Him is but the terminus after the life's walk after Him.

In a recent work of fiction there is a strange story of a wild man who went to live in a wild wood, and became the chum of a wild cat. He found the cat fast in a trap; he released it, but its leg was broken, and ever after the cat would not leave the wild man of the woods. In every incident that cat is mentioned, but always with the attention drawn to the fact that the cat "trailed a limb." If he went hunting, it went away from the man's hut "trailing a limb." When it came with its prey, it came back "trailing a limb." If it went out to look at the moon, it went "trailing a limb." That cat never turned up but it came "trailing a limb." There are a good many Christian people like that cat. Delivered? Of course they are delivered, but they "trail a limb," and that is the one thing that you always notice about them. You forget the brightness of the eyes, and the glossiness of the skin; everything is taken up with the trailing limb. A Christian man? Yes, but with a bad temper. A Christian man? Yes, but with an uncharitable spirit. A Christian man? Yes, but with what is called "an infirmity of the flesh."

There cannot be perfect soundness in the Christian life if there is any limb of the spiritual person that is trailing. But if there is any deformity He can make us whole by the thorough work of His gracious ministry. He can remove the cataract from the eye of faith, so that we can see clearly. He can cleanse the ear of heeding from the stoppage of inattention, so that it can hear responsively. He can adjust the member in the broken hand of service, so that we can work without any hindrance. He can wash the feet of our life from the pollutions of the world, so that our feet are swift and beautiful to run in His ways. He can take out the sting from an unholy tongue, so there shall drop from our lips the words which heal and help; and He can purify the heart from every contaminating thing, so that it shall be the holy place in which the Shekinah glory of His presence shall ever be shining.

The Meaning of the Spiritual Life.

II. THE " THROUGHLY " OF EQUIPPING.

The Holy Spirit after calling attention to the blessedness imported by the inspired word, says, that the practical outcome of His bestowment is that " the man of God may be perfect, *throughly* furnished unto all good works " (II. Tim. iii. 17). The Greek word rendered " *throughly furnished* " means to be perfectly fitted out. As a ship is throughly fitted out when going on a long voyage, so by the equipping power of God's Word the man of God is to be furnished for all his need. The same word as rendered " throughly furnished " is given in Acts xxi. 5, " *accomplished*," when attention is called to the fact that the apostle tarried at Tyre for seven days, and having " *accomplished* " that time he went on his way.

There are two essential things, supposing the ship is good, to make it " throughly furnished," and these are, it must be efficiently manned, and sufficiently stored.

(1) *Efficiently manned*. An efficient captain is the essentiality on board a ship, and one of the ways by which the captain's efficiency will show itself will be for him to see that his officers and crew are efficient. Admiral Blake, who was contemporary with Cromwell, was a grave and an original commander. One has said of him :

" Blake had all the moral and intellectual endowments of a great commander, either by sea or by land. A little man, broad faced, deep eyed, chary of speech, melancholy of temper, he yielded no outward gleam of brilliance. Yet British history scarcely shows a nobler character. He was loyal, unselfish, humane. He possessed the indefinable art that makes the true leader—a spell that made his men trust him, believe he could never fail, and be willing to charge with him against any odds. He was a strange compound of the prudence which calculates all the odds and the daring which scorns them. Courage with him spoke with gentle accents, and looked through quiet eyes; and yet it was as swift as Nelson's, as heroic as Ney's, as cool as Wellington's. And the key-note of Blake's character was that magnificent word *Duty*, which Nelson spelt . . . on the morning of Trafalgar, and which Henry Lawrence chose as his epitaph at Lucknow."

Personal worth and ability are traits which enabled Blake to be the man he was, but something more is needed when we come to spiritual character and work, and that something is *some one*, and that *some one* is the Holy Spirit. He is the Captain, Who is to man us, and effectually work in and through us.

The meaning of the word efficient is suggestive, it signifies the possession of power, or competency to act, effectually, that is, to bring to a successful issue. There is a word and its cognates in the New Testament which has wrapped up in it the meaning of effectual work. It is not so much the believer working as another working in him. Twice the word is used in relation to Christ. When Herod heard of the fame of Jesus, as heralded by the " mighty works " which He was doing, he came to the conclusion that John the Baptist had risen from the dead, " therefore mighty works *do shew forth in Him* " (Matt. xiv. 2), or as in the R.V., " these *powers work in Him*," or as the margin, " are *wrought* by Him." The other instance where the word occurs in relation to Christ is Eph. i. 19-20, where attention is directed to the power

The Meaning of the Spiritual Life. 41

which raised Christ from the dead—" *working* " of His mighty power, which He *wrought* in Christ when He raised Him from the dead. Effectual working is the thought in each of the references.

The reason why the Apostle Paul was the man he was, was because of the power he had, or because of the power which had him. Let us ponder a few passages where he bears testimony to this fact. [I give the word in italics, although differently rendered.] The reason why the saints at Thessalonica were the saints they were was because the word of God " *effectually worketh* " (I. Thess. ii. 13), for that word if allowed to work is always " *powerful* " (i.e., " effectual," Heb. iv. 12). The power which was to enable the Lord's people at Philippi to " work out their salvation," was " God which *worketh* in you both to will and to do of His good pleasure " (Phil. ii. 13). Paul acknowledged the power that " *wrought effectually in Peter*," but he also says, " the same *was mighty in* me " (Gal. ii. 8). The secret of his successful ministry is magnificently summed up in the following—" I also labour, striving according to His working, *which worketh in* me mightily " (Col. i. 29). The staying power which enabled him to joyfully suffer, " which," he says, " was *effectual* in the *enduring*," was because he recognised his sufferings were " the sufferings of Christ " (II. Cor. i. 5, 6). The faith which is heaven-born and acknowledged, is that which " *worketh* by love " (Gal. v. 6). We know the Lord is able to do for us " exceeding abundantly above all we ask or think," but it is only as we know the meaning of " according to the power that *worketh in* us " (Eph. iii. 20); and the apostle after enumerating the different operations of the Spirit says, "But all these *worketh*," effectually work, why? because of the Spirit Who operates (I. Cor. xii. 11). The effectual issues of the Christian life are all traced to one person, namely, the Holy Ghost.

Error is a part of truth, but I came across an error recently which is a whole truth. In Cruden's Concordance, London edition of 1835—"the tenth edition carefully revised and corrected"—Gen. xlix. 19 reads, "But *God* shall overcome at the last," whereas *Gad*, a son of Jacob, is the subject of the declaration. Here then is an error, and yet a grand and glorious truth is declared.

"God shall overcome," not like Gad, "at *the last*," but *all the time*. No power on earth, or in hell, can stay the working of His power, nor retard the might of His strength. How strong is the electric wire? As strong as the power behind it. How strong is the child of God? As strong as the Lord Himself, for He is His strength.

(2) It is necessary also for a ship, and a Christian, to be *sufficiently stored*. Miss Ellen Thorneycroft Fowler, in writing concerning *Isabel Carnaby*, represents Paul asking his father, "You have not given us your idea yet, as to what is really the name of the underlying power which leavens humanity, and which Isabel calls love, and Maderly calls beauty, and Edgar calls individualism, and I call human nature." The minister smiled. "I am an old-fashioned man, and use old-fashioned phrases," he said. "I should call it the grace of the Lord Jesus Christ." The grace of the Lord Jesus, as He said to Paul, is "sufficient." He wants everything who wants Christ. He wants nothing who has Him. The word "*sufficient*" in II. Cor. xii. 9 is translated "*enough*" in

The Meaning of the Spiritual Life. 43

Matt. xxv. 9, and "*content*" in Luke iii. 14. He who has the grace of Christ has enough to meet every emergency and is contented in consequence. Fully stored indeed is he who is stored with grace. He who knows the love of God in his heart has a satisfying portion which means enough for himself and that which contents others.

The late Dr. G. C. Lorimer has well voiced the need of the age :

"Religion is being judged by what it does, not by what it claims to be; and by what it does to-day, and not by what it may have done yesterday. That church which by its offices deepens the moral life of the community, that carries most of hope and joy to the lowly, that reclaims wanderers from God and duty, will surely attain to primacy in the new century. The picturesque, the histrionic, the archæological features of religion, and the controversies about 'orders,' 'succession,' 'vestments,' are not foremost in the thoughts of serious men to-day, and their prominence anywhere, with the noisy strife to which occasionally they give rise, strikes the modern mind as sounding brass and clanging cymbal in a world that is perishing for love."

We can only supply the needed love, as the love of God burns on the altar of our heart, and is fed by the fuel of the record of that love in the Word of God. The Word of God is not only a lamp to our feet, it is also a lighted torch to fire the wood of affection, so that the kindly word will be on the lips, the lifting help will be in the hands, the tearful sympathy will be in the eyes, the holy walk will be in the life, the gladdening joy will be in the countenance, the supplicating plea will be in the voice, and the faithful service will be in the work.

CHAPTER IV.

SCRIPTURE: THE FEEDER OF THE SPIRITUAL LIFE.

Goethe says of the Word of God—" A belief in the Bible, the fruit of deep meditations, has served me as the guide of my moral and literary life. I have found it a capital safely invested, and richly productive of interest." Every honest reader of the Word of God, and ardent believer in Christ, has found it " richly productive of interest." The Word is a *God-Transmitter*. As the atmosphere transmits the rays of the sun, so the Word of God brings the God of the Word into the heart and life, and makes them warm and luminous with the rays of His love. The Word of God is a *Christ-Revealer*. As the microscope reveals the hidden symmetrical beauty of the flower, so the Word makes known the Christ in the charm of His grace to allure and bless. The Word of God is a *Spirit-Conductor*. As the electric power communicates its energy to the car by means of the communicating wire, so the Holy Spirit is operative in us so long as we are in touch with Him by means of the Word. The Word of God is a *Life-Imparter*. As the bitten Israelites got life by means of the uplifted brazen serpent, so the Lord has ordained that spiritual life shall be imparted to us through the incorruptible and imperishable Word of His Truth. The Word of God is a *Wealth-Bestower*. As Ruth, the Moabitess, found that her union with Boaz made her a sharer of his wealth, so the Word not only gives " exceeding great and precious promises," but "all the treasures of wisdom and knowledge." The Word of God is a *Love-Inspirer*. As the love of Jonathan to David captivated him, and made him exclaim, " Thy love to me was wonderful," so the love assurances in the Word of His grace move us in the paths of sacrifice and service. And the Word of God is a *Power-Communicator*. As the woman with the issue of blood found there was power in Christ to heal her the moment she touched the hem of His garment; so those who come to the word in faith, experience the thrill of the Divine energy as it courses through the spiritual nature.

More especially, attention is directed to the controlling power of the Word of God in the inner life of the child of God, for it is as that Word controls the spiritual life, that it is strong and sure, and God is better known. Leland says,

> " When in God thou believest,
> Near God thou wilt certainly be."

We can go even further and say we are not only *near* Him, but *in* Him as we abide in His word, for He enjoins us to abide in Him, and promises through His words to abide in us. May we not say, *we only abide in Him as His words abide in us*.

" He that keepeth His commandments abideth in Him " (1. John iii. 24, R.V.).

I. AS THE SEED EMBODIES AND CONTROLS THE PLANT, SO THE WORD OF GOD ENSHRINES AND COMMUNICATES SPIRITUAL LIFE.

When visiting the St. Louis Exhibition, I saw in the Agricultural Section a life-size representation of Abraham Lincoln made out of different seeds. A man from the country, seeing it, suddenly exclaimed, "There's old Abe, made out of seed." Of every believer of Christ it must be said, "He is made of seed," not of the seed of natural life, but of the incorruptible seed of the Word of God (1. Pet. i. 23). Christ says, "The words that I speak unto you, they are spirit and life" (John vi. 63). At first glance, viewing these words in the light of their context, they seem to suggest that the words Christ speaks are to be understood spiritually, but as Professor Godet points out, there is more than this. He says, "If He said simply, ' *My words are spirit*,' one might understand these words, with Augustine, in the same sense, ' My words are to be understood spiritually.' But the second predicate : ' and life,' does not allow this explanation. The meaning is therefore : ' *My words are the incarnation and communication of the Spirit ; it is the Spirit Who dwells in them, and acts through them ; and for this reason they communicate life*.'"

The all-powerful and awe-producing fact embodied in these words of Christ is, we cannot have the Spirit nor His life apart from His Word. The "bush" of God's Word, and the living flame in it, are so one that the latter cannot be had apart from the former, any more than the plant can be apart from the seed whence it is. As we think of the seed, there are three thoughts suggested.

(1) *All that the plant will ever be is latent in the seed.*

The life-sustaining properties of the corn, the variegated beauty of the pansy, the fragrance of the rose, the blood-red colour of the poppy, the bouquet on the single stem of the fox-glove, the useful parsley, the scented thyme, and the greenness of the grass, all lie latent in the seed. Thus it is with the Word of God. When it is received into the soil of an honest heart, it soon manifests itself in the consecrated life. No sooner was the Gospel in its saving power known in Thessalonica, than there was seen the work of faith in the turning to God, the labour of love in serving the Lord, and the patience of hope in waiting for Christ (1. Thess. i. 2-10).

(2) *To make patent what is latent, the seed must be placed in a favourable environment.*

Seeds that are not planted will not grow, and seeds planted twelve inches below the surface cannot vegetate. "Some years ago a vase hermetically sealed was found in a mummy-pit in Egypt by the English traveller Wilkinson, who sent it to the British Museum. The librarian there, having unfortunately broken it, discovered in it a few grains of wheat and one or two peas, old, and wrinkled, and as hard as stone. The peas were planted carefully under glass on the 4th of June, 1844, and at the end of thirty days the seeds sprang into new life. They had probably been buried about 3,000 years, perhaps in the time of Moses." The life in the seeds was latent all that time, but it was not patent until the seeds were sown under conditions for its manifestation. The seed of the Word must be sown in the soil of faith. It will only develop in the ground of obedience. We read of some to whom it was no "profit," that is, it was no advantage to them, because it was not "mixed with faith" (Heb. iv. 2). The word "*mixed*" is the same as rendered "*tempered together*" in speaking of the union of one part of the body with the other (1. Cor. xii. 24). When the Word of God's grace is joined to the faith of our obedience, then there will be the evidence of His life. As we submit to the word's direction, it transmits the beauty of its life.

(3) *There is in the seed the possibility of endless propagation, and that possibility will become a certainty, as due attention is paid to its cultivation.*

All historians tell us that in the old times the harvests in Egypt and Syria returned an hundredfold for one, and in Babylonia two hundredfold for one. Well, suppose that I were to sow my grain in a soil as fertile as that which Egypt is said to have been in old times, my first harvest would be a hundred grains; these 100 grains would produce 100 times as much for my second harvest, or 10,000 grains; my third harvest would be 100 times 10,000, or 1,000,000 grains; and my fourth 100,000,000 grains. It has been reckoned there are about 820,000 grains in a bushel. At this rate my fourth harvest would yield about 122 bushels of grain; and four years after, it would be 100,000,000 times as much—12,200,000,000 bushels, or 1,525,000,000 quarters. This is scarcely one-sixth less than twice the 900,000,000 quarters which we reckon would be necessary to supply the whole human race for a year. Thus in eight years as much corn might spring from one seed as to supply all mankind with bread for more than a year and a half.

Without contending for, or confirming, the accuracy of the above quotation, at least one thing is demonstrated, namely, the fertility of a single grain of corn. It is a striking illustration of what we find in achievements of the Word of God. James Calvert has told us of the marvellous triumphs of the Gospel in Fiji. He says:

"There was not a single Christian in Fiji in 1835. In 1885, when the Jubilee was celebrated, there was not an avowed heathen left in all the eighty inhabited islands. There were 1,322 churches and preaching places, 10 white missionaries, 65 native ministers, 41 catechists, 1,016 teachers and preachers, 1,889 local preachers, 28,147 fully accredited church members, 4,112 on trial for membership, 3,206 class leaders, 3,069 catechumens, 2,610 scholars, and 104,585 attendants on public worship, out of a population of 110,000 !"

This, all the result of the penetrating power of the *salt* of the Gospel. It alone can season humanity and make it sweet and wholesome, as it alone can make it glad and lightsome. The results are as evident, if not more so, in the individual, for the gospel touches every part of the nature when it works unhindered. The Word is an expulsive power to turn out the tyranny of sin; an enlightening power to dispel the darkness of ignorance; an ennobling power to elevate the mind; an eradicating power to cleanse the heart; an endowing power to enrich the being, and an effectual power to bless in every way to the glory of God.

II. AS THE MOULD FORMS AND SHAPES THE METAL, SO THE WORD FORMULATES AND FASHIONS THE CHARACTER.

Walt Whitman says,

> "Charity and personal force,
> Are the only investments worth having":

Love and power are found in the Truth, and as we abandon ourselves to it, they communicate themselves to us. The apostle speaks of having "obeyed from the heart that form of doctrine" (Rom. vi. 17). The word "*form*" signifies a type, a mould, a pattern; and comes from a root which means to strike, and then as Godet says, "denotes an image deeply engraved, and fitted to reproduce its impress." The word is rendered "*print*," in speaking of the rents made by the nails in the body of Christ (John xx. 25); "*figure*" and "*pattern*," in calling attention to Adam as a type of Christ, and to the pattern of the tabernacle (Rom. v. 14; Heb. viii. 5). The phrases, "the form of doctrine" may be rendered "the example of teaching."

The greatest treatise ever written upon love is that which we find in 1. Cor. xiii., and the greatest living expression of that treatise is the Lord Jesus Himself. He answers to every trait there portrayed. Let us ponder that love as lived out by Christ, till our beings are like soft metal and run into the mould of it, then our hearts and lives shall be shaped by it. George Eliot asks the question,

"Is it what we love, or how we love,
That makes true good?"

Methinks it is *what* we love, for, as Emerson says, "Love, which is the essence of God, is not for levity, but for the total worth of man." The total worth of that love will not only form us to love like Him, but will communicate its nature to us, for it is not only a mould to shape us as we ponder the truth of it, but also a life to make us as we are swayed by it.

III. AS THE JUDGE ADJUDICATES THE CASE AND APPLIES THE LAW; SO THE WORD OF GOD DISCERNS OUR THOUGHTS AND DETERMINES OUR ACTIONS.

The Word is said to be " a discerner of the thoughts and intents of the heart " (Heb. iv. 12). The Greek word " *kritikos* " means able to judge. Many to-day are criticising the Word of God instead of being criticised by it. It alone is the judge to give a righteous judgment of our thoughts and words. The Word is always impartial in its judgment, right in its findings, and unbiassed in its actions. Ruskin says, in his *Sesame and Lilies*, in calling attention to Milton's condemnation of faithless pastors, in the following lines,—

> " Of other care they little reckoning make,
> Than how to scramble at the shearer's feast,
> *Blind mouths—*"

" This is a strange expression; a broken metaphor, one might think, careless and unscholarly. Not so; its very audacity and pithiness are intended to make us look close at the phrase and remember it.

" Those two monosyllables express the precisely accurate contraries of right character, in the two great offices of the Church, those of bishop and pastor.

" A ' Bishop ' means ' a person who oversees.'

" A ' Pastor ' means ' a person who feeds.'

" The most unbishoply character a man can have is therefore to be blind; the must unpastoral is, instead of feeding, to want to be fed—to be a *Mouth*.

" Take the two reverses together, and you have blind mouths. We may advisably follow out this idea a little. Nearly all the evils in the Church have arisen from bishops desiring power more than light. They want authority, not outlook. Whereas their real office is not to rule; though it may be vigorously to exhort and rebuke; it is the king's office to rule; the bishop's office is to oversee the flock; to number it, sheep by sheep; to be ready always to give full account of it."

I give this quotation to enforce the principle which is embodied in it, namely, no believer in Christ has a right to any name, or office unless he faithfully fulfills it. What is a believer in Christ but one who is obedient to Him? What is a branch in Christ, the Vine, but one who bears fruit by Him? What is a Christian, but one who is a representative of Christ? What is a servant of Christ, but a slave who belongs to Him? What is a child of God, but one who resembles his Father? What is a disciple, but one who follows in the steps of Christ? What is a temple, but the holy place of a sanctified heart in which the Holy Spirit dwells? This is how the Word searches us. It reminds us of what we are, that we may be what we should be.

IV. As the Food Nourishes the Body and Builds up its Tissues, so the Word gives Fibre and Muscle to our Spiritual Being, and we Become like the Food upon which we Feed.

" Man shall not live by bread alone, but by every word" (spoken word) "which proceedeth out of the mouth of God" (Matt. iv. 4). Food communicates its nutriment to the system into which it passes by means of the digestive organs, and it causes the recipient to be like itself. Buckle, in his *History of Civilization*, shows how the characters and dispositions of the various races of men are affected by the food they eat. The broad general truth of this is obvious. The gross feeders are slow thinkers. The difference between the Eskimo with his blubber, and the Englishman with his square meal, is as great as the food itself. The Scotchman owes a great deal of his sturdiness and pertinacity to the oatmeal porridge. One has well said, " We are what we are—physically, mentally, and to a great extent morally—mainly in virtue of our diet." It was not without significance that one said to another, when the other was about to partake of a certain repast, " It is not good for your morals." The same holds good in the spiritual realm. The formative as well as the feeding power of the word is beyond all question. Feed upon it, and it will be found that the feeder becomes like it. The Word does not give up its secrets nor its nourishment to the casual and careless reader. Sir Joshua Reynolds tells of the profound disappointment he felt the first time he beheld Raphael's great picture of the Transfiguration at the Vatican. It was only as he looked at it, again and again, that its grandeur and worth grew upon him. So those who ponder the Word of Truth will find the truth of the Word will impart itself; for remember, it is " a Book in cipher, which only believers can *decipher*," and they can only decipher as they are under the instruction of the Great *Decipherer*, the Holy Spirit.

V. AS THE PLAN REGULATES AND GUIDES THE BUILDER IN THE ERECTION OF A BUILDING, SO THE WORD OF GOD DIRECTS THE CONDUCT OF THE BELIEVER.

" Through faith we understand that the worlds were framed by the Word of God " (Heb. xi. 3). There are three words that we need to understand in the above verse, namely, " worlds," " framed," and " word." " *Worlds*." The word is " *æons*," which means " *ages*," and denotes the several dispensations of the world's history. Thus there is—

The Adamic age, or The period of man's innocence;

The Noahic age, or The period of man's lawlessness;

The Abrahamic age, or The period of man's pilgrimage;

The Davidic age, or The period of man's rule;

The Gentilic age, or The times of the Gentiles;

The Gospelic age, or The Dispensation of the Spirit;

The Messianic age, or The period of Israel's supremacy;

The Jehovic age, or Eternity, when God will be All in all.

"*Word.*" The word here refers to the *spoken word*, hence, it is often rendered "*saying*" as in Luke ii. 51, where we are told that Mary kept the "*sayings*" of Christ in her heart.

The word "*framed*" signifies to be in joint, to be complete; hence we read that believers should be "*perfectly joined together*" (1. Cor. i. 10), and that the disciples were "*mending*" their nets that they might be perfect (Matt. iv. 21). Taking these three words together we see at a glance that the periods which mark out the purposes of God are all based upon a plan and that that plan is made known in the spoken declaration as recorded in His written word. The plan of His thought is made known in the Word of His Grace. The same holds good as to the direction of our hearts and lives. As the ages are subservient to His plan, so should we be to His command.

CHAPTER V.

GOD: THE OBJECTIVE OF THE SPIRITUAL LIFE.

The first commandment of the Decalogue emphasizes God's claim upon His people. Like a clarion note the words ring out terse and true, "Thou shalt have none other Gods before Me" (Exod. xx. 3). Luther, in his "Table Talk," says, "I have many times essayed thoroughly to investigate the Ten Commandments, but at the very outset, 'I am the Lord thy God,' I stuck fast; that very one word, 'I,' put me to a non-plus. He that has but one word of God before him, and out of that one word cannot make a sermon, can never be a preacher." The one word to which Luther refers is only one letter, and in that personal pronoun we have brought before us the one loving and true God, whose name is "One" (Zech. xiv. 9).

The people to whom this command was given:

(1) Were saved from judgment by the blood of the paschal lamb (Exod. xii. 13; 1. Cor. v. 7).

(2) Were loved in the election of His grace (Deut. iv. 37; vii. 7, 8; x. 15; xxiii. 5; xxxiii. 3).

(3) Were called by the effectual calling of His word (Hosea xi. 1).

(4) Were delivered by the power of His redeeming hand (Deut. vii. 8; xv. 15; xxix. 25).

(5) Were protected by the bulwark of His presence (Exod. xiii. 21, 22).

(6) Were supplied by the giving from His storehouse (Neh. ix. 15).

(7) Were led by the Spirit of His power (Neh. ix. 20).

Those whom the Lord commands He first converts. He makes us His sons by His grace, and then as sons He expects us to prove our relationship by our obedience.

The first commandment *shuts out* all other gods, which means separation from idols (1. Thess. i. 9); it *shuts up* to God, which signifies consecration to Him (Rom. xii. 1); and it *shuts in* with God, which denotes fellowship with Him (Gen. vii. 16). When the Lord shut the door of the ark, He pulled it to from the inside. Those who obey the commands of the Lord can always command the Lord they obey. "Obedience is the key to every door." He who obeys shall never want a blessing, for every blessing comes to obedience. He who seeks happiness for its own sake will never find it, but he who obeys the word of the Lord will find that happiness will seek him. Obedience silences all fears, dispels all doubts, and fills the heart with contentment. As George MacDonald says: "I find the doing of the will of God, leaves me no time for disputing about His plans."

Never separate God's commands from His promises. I remember seeing in New York, just before a Presidential election, a notice setting forth the benefits which would come to the electors if they voted for a certain candidate, which announcement was in the form of a "Pod of Peas." There are five P's which the Holy Spirit has put in the Pod of His Word, and these are, precept, promise, prayer, practice, and power. Let us take Five Scriptures where the words, "*I the Lord,*" occur as fixing these five points:

(1) The straight line of His *precept*, " Ye shall be holy: for *I the Lord* your God am holy " (Lev. xix. 2).

(2) The encircling grace of His *promise*, " *I the Lord* do keep it: I will water it every moment " (Isa. xxvii. 3).

(3) The empty hand of *prayer* and the fulness of reply, " *I the Lord* will answer them " (Isa. xli. 17).

(4) The upright walk of *practice*, " Who hath wrought and done it. . . . *I the Lord*, the First and the Last. I am He. The isles saw it and feared " (Isa. xli. 4).

(5) The potent force of *power*, " The nations shall know that *I the Lord* do sanctify Israel " (Ezek. xxxvii. 28).

These five golden links form a chain which binds us to the feet of God, and will bind the world to our feet. If we fulfil the command of the Lord, He will fill to the full the promise of His Word. " The Christian life is not God *and* me: it is God *in* me." The obtainment of His power by consistent prayer is the secret to attain the direction of His Word. His precepts prompt our prayers; His promises call forth our faith; and His power enables us to carry out His commands.

There are *Three Thoughts* which are suggested by this first commandment, namely, what it excludes, what it includes, and what it concludes.

I. WHAT IT EXCLUDES.

As the idol Dagon could not stand in the presence of the ark, so the Lord will not allow " other gods " to be worshipped in addition to Him. There are many idols that are being worshipped, besides those of wood and stone.

There are many who pity the heathen idol worshipper, who have greater need to pity themselves. How many there are who bow to the golden calf, although they worship it in a more portable way than the children of Israel did! The "almighty dollar" is the one almighty to many. Righteousness, truth, honesty, and compassion are sacrificed at Mammon's shrine. There are thousands who prostrate themselves before the God Bacchus. Virtue, honour, love, and every good and noble thing are ground beneath his car. Many prostrate themselves before the goddess of unchastity, and are her helpless slaves. Others bow to the god of ceremony. Lifeless forms, bowings, eastward position, priestism, chantings, almsgiving, saints, and a hundred and one things are put in the place of Christ. When the Gospel comes in power, it revolutionizes the whole man. Reformation is not sufficient. The Dagons of idolatry must fall before the ark of God, and be not only broken but expelled and abandoned.

It is said that one of the missionaries of the China Inland Mission was the means of a large heathen temple being turned into a Christian place of worship. The missionary said after the reformation: "The temple looks very pleasant in its changed character. The two large bells now call the people to worship the living God, instead of calling the idol, as they supposed, from his feasts and slumbers. In the front temple quaint pictures of flying spirits and genii, painted on the walls, still remain. The large temple makes a very neat mission chapel, with its whitened walls and scarlet-painted posts and beams. The wooden incense table has been cut down into a preaching table, and the benches are made from the platform which supported the larger idols. On the temple front hangs a large tablet, with "Jesus Chapel" in beautiful Chinese characters, replacing the old Taoist sign. This temple now stands a distinct witness to the truth that God is a Spirit, and His glorious Gospel is proclaimed in it." The change is as distinct in the life of him who believes in the Lord Jesus. When He comes into the heart, He transforms the life. He cleanses the heart within, that He may beautify the life without.

II. WHAT DOES THIS COMMAND INCLUDE.

There is a golden thread of connected thought, found in connection with the words, "*There is none*," which brings out the inclusiveness of the being of Jehovah.

The Exclusiveness of His Being. "The Lord He is God" [Jehovah He is the Triune God]; "*there is none* beside Him*" (Deut. iv. 35).

> "There is no god, but God—to prayer—
> Lo, God is great!"

He is independent of all, but all are dependent upon Him. We cannot do without Him; He can do without us, not that He wills to. His being is proclaimed by His acting. He proclaims himself everywhere, although in the essence of His being He does not show Himself, yet as Cowper says,

> "Not a flower
> But shows some touch, in freckle, streak, or stain,
> Of His unrivall'd pencil."

The Holiness of His Nature. "*There is None* holy as Jehovah" (1. Sam. ii. 2).

"What is holiness?" was the question put by a young believer to an old one. "God is holy," was the reply. Holiness in Him is not something acquired, nor given; He is holy, hence all He does is holy, even as the rays of the sun in their warmth proclaim what the sun is. There is no rift in the lute of His character; there is no flaw in the devotion of His love; there is no fault in the consecration of His work; there is no stain in the texture of His nature; there is no alloy in the gold of His holiness; there is no spot in the sun of His testimony; and there is no crookedness in the walk of His life, for He is "glorious in holiness" (Exod. xv. 11).

The Goodness of His Character. "*There is none* good but One, that is God" (Matt. xix. 17).

Tupper, in a beautiful sentence, sums up the whole cause of God's goodness, when he says,

"God, from a beautiful necessity, is Love."

Of frequent occurrence is the statement, "*The Lord is Good.*"

His goodness is the cause of His mercy (I. Chron. xvi. 34).

His goodness is the theme of our worship (II. Chron. v. 13; vii. 3; Ezra iii. 11; Psa. c. 4; cxxxv. 3; cxxxvi. 1; Jer. xxxiii. 11).

His goodness prompts our testimony (Psa. cvi. 1, 2).

His goodness is the origin of our redemption (Psa. cvii. 1, 2).

His goodness is recognized by His servants (Psa. cxviii. 1-7).

His goodness is ministered to all (Psa. cxlv. 9).

His goodness is the cause of answered prayer (Lam. iii. 25).

His goodness is the stronghold for our protection (Nah. i. 7).

Christ "went about doing good" (Acts x. 38). Being Who He was, He was Good going about. His good was all good, and always good. We cannot be as good as He, any more than a rushlight can be the sun, but we can shine with the light we have. Happy shall we be if we can say, by the grace of God, with John Wesley at last, "Eighty-seven years have I sojourned on this earth, endeavouring to do good."

The Provision of His Salvation. "Look unto Me, and be ye saved .... for I am God, and *there is none else*" (Isa. xlv. 22). "*There is none* other name .... whereby we must be saved" (Acts iv. 12). These terse and telling statements shut us up to the Lord Himself if we would be saved. Pascal tersely says :—

"All those who seek God apart from our Lord Jesus Christ, and stop short in nature, either feel no light which satisfies them, or work out for themselves, without a mediator, an imperfect system of knowing and serving God, and hence they fall into atheism, or deism, two errors equally abhorent to the Christian religion. Without Jesus Christ, the world could not subsist."

A poor blind man on London Bridge, reading an embossed Bible, lost his place, as he was reading the words, "*None other name.*" Some of the people smiled as he kept repeating, "None other name"; but one who was passing heard the words, and they kept ringing in his ears. He was trying to save himself, and had failed in the attempt. The chimes from the bells, the singing of the birds, all seemed to say, "None other name." At last he was able to rest in Him Who bears the name of names. "I see it all," he said. "I see it all. I have been trying to be saved by my own works—my repentance, my prayers, my reformation. I see my mistake. It is Jesus Who alone can save me. To Him I will look. Neither is there salvation in any other: for there is none other name under Heaven given among men whereby we must be saved."

The Sovereignty of His Grace. "*There is none* else," again and again the Spirit plays upon this string of the violin of His Word; no less than nine times in two chapters (Isa. xlv. 5, 6, 14, 18, 21, 22; xlvi. 9), when he calls attention to the fact that He alone can bless. The cause of our blessing is in Himself.

When one sought to explain away the sovereignty of His grace in His electing love to an old Christian, she aptly replied: "If He had not chosen me before I was, I am sure He would not have chosen me after." Or as another said: "I don't know why He loved me, but I suppose He loved me because He would love me."

The Hopelessness of Man's Need. Like a death knell the solemn chime rings out in the Belfry of God's Word, as it calls attention to man's hopelessness, helplessness and homelessness—"*There is none !*" Listen to the dreadful chime!

"*There is none* that doeth good" (Psa. xiv. 1).

"*There is none* to help" (Psa. xxii. 11).

"*There is none* that can deliver" (Isa. xliii. 13).

The Objective of the Spiritual Life. 63

"*There is none* to guide" (Isa. li. 18).

"*There is none* to raise" (Amos v. 2).

"*There is none* upright" (Micah vii. 2).

"*There is none* warm" (Hag. i. 6).

"*There is none* righteous" (Rom. iii. 10).

"*There is none* that understandeth" (Rom. iii. 11).

"*There is none* that seeketh God" (Rom. iii. 11).

There is none on earth, but there is One in Heaven, and from Heaven. One of these "There is none" applies to Him. He said in His aloneness on the cross, "*There is none* to help" (Psa. xxii. 11). Because there was none to deliver Him, He can help us. Earth has no sorrows that Heaven cannot cure, but Heaven alone can. There are two "spent all's" in the Gospel of Luke. The woman with the issue of blood "spent all" she had in trying to get better of the disease which was draining away her life; and the prodigal "spent all" he had in frittering away his substance. But when each of these came to the source of Divine power, they both of them got blessed. Remember, as Lowell says,

> " 'Tis Heaven alone that is given away,
> 'Tis only God can be had for the asking."

III. WHAT DOES THIS COMMAND CONCLUDE?

The conclusion to which faith comes is *not to have any other god but the Lord*. The words," No other gods before Me," mean *in addition to Me*. What does this signify practically?

It means to respond to Him fully. The Lord said to Abram, "Walk before *Me*, and be thou perfect" (Gen. xvii. 1).

For thirteen years Abram had been walking before Sarah, in listening to her as to the obtaining of the promised seed. All these years there had been no revelation from God, as may be gathered by comparing Gen. xvi. 16 and xvii. 1. Then the Lord reveals Himself as *the Almighty God* (The-many-breasted-God, i.e., the all-sufficient-One); and bids him cease his scheming and be upright, for He was well able to fulfil His promise. Abram does as the Lord wishes and is blessed as a result.

To serve the Lord faithfully. "I have seen thee righteous before *Me*," was the Lord's word to Noah; and from the Epistle to the Hebrews we know that he, "being wary" (margin) of the Lord's command to fulfil it, was commended for his faithfulness (Gen. vii. 1; Heb. xi. 7). Faithfulness means two things, being full of faith to believe all God says, and then to carry out in every detail all He commands, regardless of consequences. As Emerson says, "What I must do is all that concerns me, not what people think"; for remember, "God estimates us not by the position we are in, but by the way in which we fill it."

> "Let the road be rough and dreary,
> And its end far out of sight,
> Foot it bravely strong or weary,
> Trust in God and do the right."

To love the Lord supremely. It is only whole-hearted love that can say to the Lord, "Whom have I in Heaven but thee?" (Psa. lxxiii. 25).

There are *three traits*, among others, *of love :* (1) True love is *pure* in its affection, for it loves for love's sake; (2) it is *sacrificing* in its giving, for it is more concerned about others than itself; (3) and it is *ardent* in its feeling, for it ever expresses itself with warmth. The Hebrew slave showed his love for his master, by sacrificing his liberty, and serving him for love's sake (Exod. xxi. 5, 6). We know love by its acting not by its talking. Sydney Smith has ironically said, "You find people ready enough to do the good Samaritan—*without the oil and twopence!*" Not so with love, it spends and is spent (II. Cor. xii. 15).

To obey the Lord unhesitatingly. There are *three kinds of obedience.* There is a *tardy obedience* which acts because of the presence of the law of necessity, like Jonah, who went to Nineveh when forced by his experience in the sea-monster; there is an *argumentative obedience* which hesitates before it responds, like Peter when the Lord told him to cast the net into the sea, but instead of responding heartily, tells the Lord practically it would be useless, as he and those with him had been doing that all night; and there are those who obey the Lord *promptly,* like Philip when he was told to leave the revival in Samaria and go to speak to one man in the desert. Hesitation and vacillation often bring consternation, while promptness and readiness always secure benediction. Let us ever pray with Herbert, as to our obedience,

"Touch it with Thy celestial quickness."

To realise the Lord consciously. " I have set the Lord always before me " (Psa. xvi. 8), says the Psalmist. The mystics speak of "*practising the presence of God.*" "Are you alone, Miss?" said a man to a young lady as she was walking along a country road one evening.

"No," was the prompt reply. "I do not see anyone with you," was the rejoinder. "Indeed, sir," she said, "there is; the Lord Jesus is with me." "I beg your pardon," he immediately exclaimed; "I was not aware you kept such good company." The company of Christ is the best company, for it means *cheer in sadness*, as the two journeying to Emmaus found (Luke xxiv. 32); it is *calm in storm*, as the apostle experienced in the ship (Acts xxvii. 23); it is *companionship in loneliness*, as Paul found when he had no earthly friend to stand by him (II. Tim. iv. 17); it is *courage in distress*, as Joseph knew (Gen. xxxix. 2, 3, 21, 23); it is *confidence in conflict*, as David testified when he went against Goliath (I. Sam. xvii. 45); it is *communion in sorrow*, as the sisters at Bethany discovered when Jesus wept with them (John xi. 34, 35); and it is the *cure-all for all care*, as Moses found when the Lord said, "My presence shall go with thee" (Exod. xxxiii. 14). If we recognise the promise of His Word, we shall realise the power of His presence.

To trust the Lord implicitly. What a difference there is between the "we are not able" of the unbelieving spies, and the "we are able" of the men of faith (Num. xiii. 33). The first see themselves as grasshoppers (Num. xiii. 33), and the others see their enemies as the Lord sees them—"Grasshoppers" (Isa. xl. 22).

Unbelief asks the question, "Can God?" Faith bears the testimony, "God can." Faith does not question, it quietly rests. Faith goes forward at the Lord's command: unbelief at its own suggestion goes back. Unbelief says, "There are lions in the way"; faith sings, "I fear no foe with Thee at hand to bless."

The Objective of the Spiritual Life.

Unbelief asks, " How can these things be ? " Faith says, " He says they can be, and they are."

> " Faith is the subtle chain
> Which binds us to the Infinite : the voice
> Of a deep life within, that will remain
> Until we crowd it thence."

To possess the Lord empoweringly. When we have got into the position of Jehoshaphat and confess we have " no might," then the Lord can make us know that " to them that have 'no might' He increaseth strength " (II. Chron. xx. 12 ; Isa. xl. 29). We are often anxious to possess the *power* of God, but we are not so keen to possess the *God* of power. If He had more of us we should have more of Him.

A beautiful story is told of Princess Alice, the daughter of Queen Victoria. An old woman in Darmstadt was in receipt of 6d. per week from the parish. The Princess heard of her, went often to see her, and always brought her some present. At last, one day, overcome with gratitude, the old woman ventured to enquire, " And who is the lady to whom I am indebted for all this exceeding kindness ? " The Princess replied : " I myself am nobody, but my mother is the Queen of England." So says the true servant of Christ as to his power, as Paul did, " I be nothing " ; yet we can always say with him, " I can do all things in Christ Who strengtheneth " (II. Cor. xii. 11 ; Phil. iv. 13).

The practical lesson suggested by the Commandment is, The Lord claims all because He is All.

Mr. Spurgeon once said that some professing Christians reminded him of jerry-built houses which he had seen ; " they were Queen Anne in front and Mary

Ann behind." It is not so with possessing believers, they give Him all, for they recognise with Ruskin, "He who offers God a second place, offers Him no place at all."

> "Thou, my All.
> My Theme, my inspiration and my Crown.
> My Strength in Age. My Rise in low Estate.
> My soul's Ambition, Pleasure, Wealth, my World.
> My Light in darkness, and my Life in death.
> My Boast through time, Bliss through eternity.
> Eternity, too short to speak Thy praise,
> Or fathom Thy profound of love to man."

CHAPTER VI.

LOVE: THE HEART OF THE SPIRITUAL LIFE.

"The love of Christ constraineth us" (II. Cor. v. 14).

George Eliot says: "What makes life dreary is the want of motive."

I venture to differ from the gifted authoress; it is not "the want of motive," but the want of a true motive, which "makes life dreary" and unworthy. *Love of money* sways the coveteous man like the wind-bent hedge. *Love of place*, like the hunger of the jackal, actuates the ambitious man. *Love of self*, like the killing parasite, dominates the selfish man. *Love of pleasure*, like the fabled siren, attracts the worldly man. *Love of lust*, like the consuming fire, burns up the sensual man. *Love of humanity*, like the Good Samaritan, moves the philanthropic man; but *the love of Christ*, like a pressing crowd without and a burning fever within, presses and fires the truly Christian man.

The Greek word rendered "*constraineth*" in the text is translated "*throng*" in describing the throng of people surrounding Christ on one occasion, which is more strikingly put in the R.V., "The multitude press Thee and crush Thee"; and the same word is rendered "holden" when attention is drawn to the fact that Peter's wife's mother was held by a burning fever (Luke iv. 38; viii. 45). If the love of Christ is an inspiring force within and a protecting environment without, we shall indeed know that the Christian life is a love-inspired life.

I. THE GREATEST WANT OF THE AGE IS THE WANT OF PERSONAL ACQUAINTANCE WITH THE LOVE OF CHRIST.

Robert Browning, in one of his poems, asks the question, " Wanting is what ?" as he was looking around on a perfect summer's day. It was bliss to be alive, and yet there was something missing.

> " Wanting is what ?
> Summer redundant,
> Blueness abundant,
> Where is the spot ?
> Beamy the world, yet
> A blank all the same."

There is a want everywhere if Christ is wanted, but when He is supplied every want is met.

> " Thou, O Christ, art all I want,
> More than all in Thee I find."

We may well pray, if we do not possess Him,—

> " Come Thou, complete incompletion, O Comer,
> Pant through the blueness, perfect the summer."

Religious ordinances may be observed, but unless we have Christ in them they are a dead form. There is plenty of *I*anity to-day, but very little *Christ*ianity. Many observe a ritual who do not know the realities of the truth. The doctrines of the gospel are not dogmas to be formulated into a creed, but the directions of the Christ, to be obeyed without a question. A lunatic, on one occasion, was found sitting at a table with an empty plate before him, and holding a knife and fork. He made a pretence of eating. A friend asked him, " What are you doing ?" " I am going through the motions," was the reply. *Motions* indeed, that was all. That madman was more sane than some sane people, who imagine that the observance of outward things is of any consequence unless the inward realities are known. With some of the deductions and inductions of Marie Corelli we have no sympathy, but we have the greatest sympathy when she says: "Let not the unfaithful think that because they say long prayers, or go regularly and devoutly to church with meek faces and piously folded hands, that the eternal Wisdom is deceived thereby." The gifted authoress is referring to one of her characters, whose wife had been diabolically untrue to him, and whose unfaithfulness had been discovered by him.

He says of her: "My wife could pray—she could kneel like a lovely saint in the dim religious light of the sacred altars, her deep eyes upturned to the blameless, reproachful Christ—and, look you, each word she uttered was a blasphemy, destined to come back on herself as a curse. Prayer is dangerous for liars—it is like falling wilfully on an upright naked sword."

These are burning words, which scorch all of us, and I only quote them that we may be driven back upon this fact, "That any salvation," as George MacDonald says, "short of knowing God, is no salvation at all." *Moral Maxims may be followed, but they are dry roots, and not living regulators, apart from Christ.*

Longfellow says:

"Morality without religion" (I prefer to say "without Christ") "is only a kind of dead reckoning—an endeavour to find our place on a cloudy sea by measuring the distance we have run, but without observation of the heavenly bodies."

Dead reckoning is not sure ground. He only is sure who adjusts the sextant of his heart's faith to the Sun of Heaven's light. "He who builds beneath the sky builds too low." The mere endeavour to follow the most perfect being who has ever lived upon this earth will only end in failure. The imitation of Christ can only be accomplished as we have the indwelling of Christ. We need to have Him living within us as the Power, that we may know that we are copying Him as our Pattern. The reproduction of the perfect life of Christ, in any degree, is only possible as He lives in our hearts and is the Reproducer of that life Himself."

"I want a horse, Pa," said a wee chap to his father. "What kind of a horse, my boy?" replied the father, "a wooden horse?" "No, Pa, I want a horse." "Do you mean an iron horse?" "No, I want a horse, a horse made of horse." He wanted the reality, not an imitation. So man, in the heart-hunger of his need, cries, "I want the Christ, not the wooden Christ of a lifeless ritual, nor the iron Christ of moral maxims, but the living, loving, liberating, lifting Christ of Galilee, Gethsemane, Calvary, Olivet, and God's Throne."

Social improvements may be inaugurated, but unless the individual is improved by the touch of faith in Christ, there is nothing but a dead body wanting a living soul. The soul of improvement is the improvement of the soul. Sanitation is not regeneration. Clean houses are good, but clean hearts are better. White-wash is essential to health, but being washed white is the essence of salvation. A good environment is an important factor; but what use is it to a dead body? It only makes a good environment bad. By all means abolish unsanitary dwellings, stamp out houses of ill-fame, have good laws on the Statute Book, educate the young, provide facilities for improving the mind, give an adequate wage for service rendered, have open spaces that God's air may be breathed, light up with electric lamp the dark places where evil plies her trade, let the people say whether the dram-shops shall be or not; but these are not all. They deal with earth, not with heaven; with time, not with eternity; with the exterior, not the interior; with the body, not with the man. Put God's first, first—" Seek ye first the kingdom of God and His righteousness "; and if this is done, everything else will fall into its right place. Men get wrong with men, because they are not right with God. Love to Christ always proves itself by love to man.

The late Dr. J. C. Lorimer has rightly voiced the true order of things when he says:

"While the Church may give her support to special measures of reform, and should always do so when they are sound, it is Her purpose and plan to begin, not on the surface, but at the root of things; not on the effects, but the causes; not on the external crystallization and organization of human infirmity and moral weakness, but on the internal, on the heart from whence they spring. Her theory is: cleanse the sources, and the river will be pure; maintain the power in the power-house, and the traffic will keep on the move; supply and fill the reservoir, and the homes of the citizens will not lack for water. This is her supreme object. Hence, her belief in spiritual renewals; hence her constant and varied endeavours to get at the individual, at the conscience."

II. THE LOVE OF CHRIST IS THE INSPIRING FORCE OF THE CHRISTIAN LIFE.

> "Life, with all it yields of joy or woe,
> And hope and fear . . . .
> Is just our chance o' the prize learning love."

What love? Whose love? The love of Christ. His love is the only love that is full of disinterestedness. There is no alloy of self, nor dross of unholy passion in the pure flame of His affection. Let us ponder some of the traits of that love, as it has, does, and will work out in the lives of those who abandon themselves to Him, Who is the fountain of it, and Who lives in the flow of its moving force.

(1) *The Love of Christ! Sacrifice is its Meaning.*

"The Son of God Who loved me, and gave Himself for me" (Gal. ii. 20). When Christ loved, He gave. Love, like the sun shining in its warmth, ever gives itself in warm action; unlike mere sentiment which, like the moon in itself, is cold and barren. As when the woman touched the hem of Christ's garment, the life which was in Him coursed through the whole of her being; so the love of Christ, when He in His love is known, causes the one who knows that love to sacrifice too. There is no greater example of this than the Apostle Paul. In speaking of his life's labours, and what he was willing to do, in writing to the Church at Corinth, he says: "I will very gladly spend and be spent for you" (II. Cor. xii. 15). The words "spend" and "spent" are most significant. The first refers to his giving away what he had, like the prodigal and the diseased woman who spent all their substance, the one in riotous living and the other in getting medical advice to get rid of her malady. The substance of each was entirely consumed. The word "*spent*" refers to physical exhaustion; yea, the life itself given up in serving others. It means to be spent out, like a spent bullet which cannot go further. This is what love does; it is not concerned about itself, nor its means, so long as it can serve.

> "Through death the world is raised above
> Its alien curse and kindred dust;
> We on the cross read God is just,
> But in the offering, God is love."

> "From death comes life. The hand of God
> This direst curse to good transforms;
> So purest air is born of storms;
> So bursts the harvest from the clod.
> The highest benedictions hide
> Where sacrifice is pure and true;
> And our poor self-denials, too,
> If done for Christ, in Him abide."

(2). *The Love of Christ! Righteousness is its Principle.*

A threefold designation of love, in that treatise of treatises on its character is, " Taketh not account of evil, rejoiceth not in unrighteousness, but rejoiceth with the truth " (1. Cor. xiii. 5, 6, R.V.).

Christ could not, and would not, demean Himself to mean actions. Evil had no recognition from Him, unrighteousness fled from His presence, and truth was the one thing He was and did. Love does not take advantage of another's ignorance, nor sell one article at two prices, nor pass off linsey-woolsey for wool, nor misrepresent, nor say a thing that means one thing to him who says it, and said in such a way as to give a different meaning to the hearer.

Those who know the love of Christ, not only do to others as they would be done by, but do to others as He would do to them.

(3) *The Love of Christ! Disinterestedness is its Character.*

The tersest commentary and the fullest summary of the life of Christ is given us in the following words: "He went about doing good." He did good, not in order to get good, nor to get a good name, nor a reputation for being good, but because He was good and delighted to do it. Love acts in a corresponding way; hence, any action without love is a mere noise—a clanging cymbal.

> "Though I lavish'd all I have
>   On the poor in charity;
> Though I shrank not from the grave,
>   Or unmoved the stake could see;
> Though my body here were given
>   To the all-consuming flame—
> If my mind were still the same,
>   Meeter were I not for Heaven,
> Till by love my works were crown'd,
> Till in love my strength was found."

No truer or more trenchant words have been uttered than those by the apostle of political economy and disinterestedness, I refer to Ruskin. He says, in emphasising the principle, that men should do right because it is right, and not because of what they get:

" The soldier must die rather than forsake the ranks; the pastor starve rather than preach with flattering tongue; the physician risk the deadliest disease rather than fly from the plague; the lawyer sacrifice brief and fee rather than countenance injustice; and the merchant and the manufacturer suffer bankruptcy rather than adulterate their provisions or provide for the public inadequate or destructive material."

He also says:

"With all brave and rightly-trained men their work is first, their fee second. But in every nation there are a vast class who are ill-educated, cowardly, and, more or less, stupid. And with these people, just as certainly the fee is first, and the work second, as with brave people the work is first and the fee second. And this is no small distinction. It is the whole distinction in a man—distinction between life and death in him, between heaven and hell for him. You cannot serve two masters; you must serve one or the other. If your work is first with you and your fee second, work is your master, and the Lord of work, Who is God. But if your fee is first with you, and your work second, fee is your master, and the lord of fee, who is the devil."

(4) *The Love of Christ! Help is its Occupation.*

One of the most pertinent and practical questions asked in the Bible is, "Whoso hath the world's goods, and beholdeth his brother in need, and shutteth up his compassion from him, how doth the love of God abide in him?" (1. John iii. 17, R.V.). To say well and act ill, to plan and not to perform, to have a benevolent face and not a helping hand, is to prove we are hollow, hard, and selfish.

When Dr. Guthrie wanted his ragged schools founded he called on a certain minister, who said, "Well, you know, Mr. Guthrie, there is nothing very new in your scheme ; I and Mr. So-and-So have been thinking over a similar plan to yours for the last twenty years." " Oh, yes," replied Dr. Guthrie, " I dare say ; but you have never carried it out." So some people are always thinking over some plan of their own, but while the grass grows the steed starves. They think and talk, but do not act and help.

Love is not like this. Love acts. It sees the need and supplies it ; it beholds the helplessness and stretches forth its hand to save ; it is careless about its own comfort, but it is careful about the comfort of others. Love weeps with the sorrowful, goes after the erring, succours the needy, cheers the faint, heartens the discouraged, brightens the depressed, and cheers the despondent. Love does not patronise, it provides. Love does not do for fame or gain, but for love's sake. Love has a fire for the cold body, a bed for the destitute, a meal for the hungry, a warm heart for the rejected, a helping hand for the sinking, and a soul to feel.

(5) *The Love of Christ ! Holiness is its Life.*

Pope says : " Worth makes the man " ; and Walt. Whitman declares, " Charity and personal force are the only investments worth anything." Christ's worth and personal force are both wrapped up in His love. What a person is, gives value to what he does, and makes it an influence for good. Every trait of love spoken of in 1. Corinthians xiii. is portrayed in Christ. If we would be like Christ in the purity of His heart, in the unsullied righteousness of His actions, in the spotlessness of His character, in the beauty of His moral perfection, in the glow of His ardent grace, in the tenderness of His compassion, and in the delight of His doing of the will of God, then our heart's affection must be lighted by, and fed with, the fuel of His love. And that love will burn up every evil thing and make us, as the Irish boy said, when he was asked what holiness was, " Clean inside " ; and not only clean inside but holy outside ; that is, our lives will correspond to Christ, even as the leaf of the tree bears upon it the shape and make of the tree itself.

(6) *The Love of Christ ! Sympathy is its Feeling.*

Keble aptly voices the sympathy of Christ :

> " Thou wilt feel all, that Thou mayest pity all.
> He to earth's lowest cares is still awake."

And Whittier is in unison :

> " But warm, sweet, tender, even yet
>   A Present Help is He ;
> And faith has still its Olivet ;
>   And Love its Galilee.
> The healing of His seamless dress,
>   Is by our beds of pain ;
> We touch Him in Life's throng and press,
>   And we are whole again."

If we know His sympathy we shall be sympathetic, for as George MacDonald says, " When God comes to man, man looks round for his neighbour." And looks round with a heart of sympathy. The helping hand is no hand of real help unless it is warmed with the heart of feeling. " To be mighty of heart, mighty of mind, is to be great in life. To give alms is nothing, unless we give thought too, and therefore it is written, not blessed is he that feedeth the poor, but blessed is he that considereth the poor."

(7) *The Love of Christ! Christ is its Embodiment.*

If we would love like Christ, we must know Him personally, and allow His love to come into our nature. If every evil love is to be exterminated, and every true love is to be sanctified, He must in His love live in our hearts.

There is no power so moving and so making as the Love of Christ, and that love as exhibited on Calvary. "I stood," says one, "before that gospel in colour, ' The Descent from the Cross,' in a foreign art gallery. Many came and went, giving but a careless gaze. One aged woman I saw standing before the canvas who seemed riveted to the spot, as Mary to the Crucified. She gazed and wept. Her trembling lips were more eloquent than speech. She had eyes to see; they were her affections. The treasures of Jesus' love and grace were hidden to others; but to her, He was the chiefest among ten thousand, and the altogether lovely."

Do you know this love of Christ? Is it a power in your heart and life? Does it move and mould you? If not, why not? Seek that love. Seek Him Who is the Living Expression of the Love of God. Then life will be lived, as His life was—for others, for God.

CHAPTER VII.

HOLINESS: THE SANCTITY OF THE SPIRITUAL LIFE.

There are two sides to the subject of holiness: what believers are in Christ, and what Christ can be in the believer. The former is what might be called *positional* holiness; and the latter, *practical* holiness. The first is perfect and complete, the second is definite and progressive.

Positional holiness depends upon God Himself by means of the atonement of Christ (Heb. x. 10), and refers to our place in Christ, as sanctified (1. Cor. i. 2), accepted (Eph. i. 6), perfected (Heb. x. 14), and complete in Him (Col. ii. 10). Hence it is said, we "are sanctified" (1. Cor. vi. 11), "made meet" (Col. i. 12), and as Christ is (1. John iv. 17).

Practical holiness is the one thing I emphasise in this study. The question is frequently asked, "What is holiness?" and many are the answers which are given in the noisy atmosphere of the babel of religious tongues. If we would have a definite and clear answer we must calmly come to the sacred shrine of the Holy Scriptures, and listen to the voice of the Lord as He speaks to us therein. I propose therefore giving a sixfold answer, as found in the pages of Holy Writ, to the question, What is holiness?

I. SEPARATION TO THE LORD.

The primary meaning of the word to sanctify is to separate; hence we read, "God blessed the seventh day and sanctified it" (Gen. ii. 3); i.e., set it apart as a day of rest. The Tabernacle, after it was finished, was sanctified, viz., set apart as a dwelling place for Jehovah (Exod. xxix. 43). There are many uses of the word, but in each there is the thought of separation. The nation of Israel was set apart from the rest of the nations as God's chosen people (Exod. xxxiii. 16); the firstborn of Israel was set apart as the Lord's special portion from the rest of the nation (Exod. xiii. 2); Aaron and his sons were set apart for the priesthood, to do service for the Lord in the Tabernacle (Exod. xxviii. 41); David dedicated (set apart) all the silver and gold he had taken as spoils of war to the Lord (II. Sam. viii. 11); Jeremiah was set apart to his prophet's office by the Lord (Jer. i. 5); the cities of refuge were sanctified as places of safety for the manslayer (Josh. xx. 7, margin); and the year of Jubilee was sanctified as a special time of blessing (Lev. xxv. 10).

There is one incident in the life of Hezekiah which illustrates the meaning of sanctification. When he came to the throne things were in a very corrupt state. One of the first things he did was to charge the Levites to cleanse the House of the Lord. They obeyed, for they "cleansed all the House of the Lord," recovered the vessels of the sanctuary which had been "put away" by King Ahaz, and said, "We have prepared and sanctified"; and they did their work thoroughly for their action is contrasted with that of the priests, for it is said, "The Levites were more upright in heart to sanctify themselves than the priests" (II. Chron. xxix. 5, 15, 18, 34). Their act of sanctification meant two things: the unclean separated from the House of the

The Sanctity of the Spiritual Life.

Lord, and the dedication to Him in whole-hearted surrender and service.

Separation for separation's sake is nothing more or less than Phariseeism, which is self-righteousness; but separation to the Lord means contact with the Holy One, and is the communication of His holiness to us, just as the moment the sacrifice touched the altar it was sanctified (Exod. xxix. 37).

There must be no keeping back part of the price as Ananias did, no spirit of reluctance in surrender, or the sacrifice is marred. We must not be like the boy, whose father had given him a sixpence and a penny, telling him he might put one or the other in the contribution plate. "Which did you give?" his father asked, when the boy came home. "Well, father, I thought at first I ought to put in the sixpence, but then just in time I remembered, 'The Lord loveth the cheerful giver,' and I knew I could give the penny a great deal more cheerfully, so I put that in." Giving after such a manner is not giving in the Lord's estimation.

The one thing which will make us separate ourselves willingly to the Lord is to know the Lord to Whom we separate.

There is an incident in the history of Scotland that has exercised a strange power over the minds of the people for more than a hundred and fifty years. I refer to the revival to Charles Stuart in 1745, and the rallying of the chieftains to his standard. It is related of Lochiel that he had no faith in the enterprise, and that he informed his brother that he would go and expostulate with the prince. His brother's advice was: "Go not near the prince, for so fascinating is the power of his person that he will toss your mind like a feather in the wind, and you will be unable to do what you wish." Lochiel, however, would not be dissuaded. He went and saw the prince, who listened patiently to his remonstrance, and then replied: "My father has often told me how that Lochiel in the days gone by hath done brave things for his king, and to-morrow the standard will be raised, and you will go to your home and at your fireside will learn the fortunes or fate of your prince."

Then the chieftain, deeply moved, answered: "The standard will be raised, and I will be there, and every man of my clan will pour out to the last drop his blood for his prince."

The sight of our Prince will captivate us and win our hearts to Himself. The attractiveness of Christ will eclipse the attractions of earth, yea, He outweighs the bliss of Heaven. As Rutherford once said, "He Himself is more excellent than Heaven." There will be no more difficulty to be separated to Himself, when He is known after such a fashion, than there is for us to keep on the earth by the force of the law of gravitation.

> "Who would be cleansed from every sin,
>   Must to God's holy altar bring
> The whole of life—its joys and tears,
> Its hopes, its loves, its powers, its years,
>   The will, and every cherished thing!
> Must make this sweeping sacrifice—
>   Choose God, and dare reproach and shame,
>   And boldly stand in storm or flame
> For Him Who paid redemption's price;
> Then trust (not struggle to believe),
>   And trusting wait, nor doubt, but pray
>   That in His own good time He'll say,

' Thy faith hath saved thee ; now receive.'
His time is when the soul brings all,
   Is all upon His altar lain ;
   When pride and self-conceit are slain,
And crucified with Christ, we fall
Helpless upon His Word, and lie :
   Then, faithful to His word, we feel
   The cleansing touch, the Spirit's seal,
And know that He doth sanctify."

II. CLEANSING BY THE LORD.

If there is one thing more than another which the Lord abominates it is uncleanness. The foul breath of worldliness, the gangrene of impure desire, the slime of pride, the canker of covetousness, the rust of selfishness, the mould of envy, and the ferment of hate, are hateful things in the sight of the Lord ; hence He bids us " cleanse ourselves from all filthiness of the flesh and spirit, perfecting holiness in the fear of the Lord."

There are three words in the New Testament translated "*pure*." One of the words signifies the genuineness of any given thing. It signifies that which has been judged by the sunlight, and so found to be genuine. This word is rendered " *pure* " and " *sincere* " (II. Pet. iii. 1 ; Phil. i. 10). Another word denotes that which is clean, chaste, not contaminated by anything evil, free from defilement. It is translated " *clear* " (II. Cor. vii. 11) ; " *chaste* " (I. Pet. iii. 2) ; and " *pure* " (II. Tim. ii. 22). The third word signifies that which is pure from everything that would change or corrupt the nature of the subject with which it is combined ; that is, free from every foreign admixture.

A simple illustration will show us the progressive meaning of these three words. Suppose we take a gold coin of the realm. We test it and, being gold, it stands the test and proves that it is a genuine coin. But as we examine it we find there is dirt between the letters of marking. We wash it thoroughly with a cleansing fluid; now it is not only a genuine coin, it is also a clean one. Let us go a step farther; we get a chemist to analyse the mineral of the coin, and we find there is a small quantity of alloy with the gold, so that the coin is not absolutely pure gold. These three illustrations illustrate the three meanings of the word "pure"; and may be applied to believers. Every true believer in Christ has the genuine coin of new life in Christ; but it is necessary that the face of the outward and inward life should be cleansed from all defilement—"cleansed from all filthiness of the flesh and of the spirit" (II. Cor. vii. 1). Yet there is something higher and grander than this, namely, "perfecting holiness in the fear of the Lord." The inner shrine of the heart is to be pure, that we may have the beautiful vision of God (Matt. v. 8).

Love, like the transmitter of the wireless telegraphy, is to be received by the receiver of a "pure heart" (I. Tim. i. 5), for love can only do its work as the heart is in a right state. The secret of prevailing prayer is to "call on the Lord out of a pure heart" (II. Tim. ii. 22), for prayer can only prevail, as the plant can only flourish, when found in a right environment. If the pure gold of His grace and the pure river of His Spirit blesses us, then like the "pure gold" of the Heavenly Jerusalem and the "pure river," we shall reflect the glory of God (Rev. xxi. 18; xxii. 1), for the garment of our life will be "clean" (Rev. xix. 8).

I fancy I hear some one say, " Such purity is impossible." Yes, from the human standpoint, but not from the Divine. The main proposition is, not cleansing for the Lord, but "*by*" Him. He can do what we cannot. When the Chicago river was such a pest because of its sluggish flow into Lake Michigan, a scheme was devised to cut a channel into the Des Plaines river, which in turn flows into the mighty Mississippi. Then Lake Michigan, instead of receiving the pestilential water, was the means of cleansing out its bed and making it a blessing instead of a curse. So when the life that is resident in our Divine Head courses through our spiritual being, He not only cleanses us, but keeps us clean.

III. HOLINESS IS ADJUSTMENT IN THE LORD.

The Apostle Paul in closing his second epistle to the church at Corinth gave a parting wish and a pressing command. The wish was, " we wish your perfection "; and the command was, " Be perfect " (II. Cor. xiii. 11). There were many elements in the church at Corinth which were anything but helpful to the deeper life. There was the *unholy wedge of division*, which had pried open the door of their communion to its disturbance; there was the *morphia of slumber* which had soothed them to sleep; there was the *big head of pride* which was evidenced in their being " puffed up "; and there was the *blight of self-sufficiency* which had settled upon them, and made them question the authority of the apostle's teaching. Hence there was a needs be that they should be adjusted.

The word "*perfect*," in the above command, means

to be in joint. It is rendered "*mending*" in calling attention to the disciples' mending their nets (Matt. iv. 21); "*fitted*," in speaking of those who have made themselves objects of wrath by their sins (Rom. ix. 22); "*restore*," in urging the duty incumbent upon those who are spiritual to restore an erring brother (Gal. vi. 1); "*prepared*," in referring to Christ's body—"a body hast Thou prepared me" (Heb. x. 5); and "*framed*," in proclaiming Christ as the great Architect of the ages (Heb. xi. 3). To be perfect means to be fully answering to the Divine ideal in our Christian experience, so that we are fitted for His use, because we are in joint with Himself. The same word is given in 1. Cor. i. 10, "*perfectly joined together*." As a broken, or dislocated limb causes the body to be imperfect, so if there is any want of answering to the will of God, there is imperfection on our part. This does not signify the sinless perfection of the believer, but it does declare what we find in the Word of God, namely, "a conscience void of offence" (Acts xxiv. 16), knowing nothing against oneself (1. Cor. iv. 4, R.V.), a blameless life (1. Thess. v. 23), being full grown (Eph. iv. 13), doing the will of God (1. John ii. 17), walking in the Spirit (Gal. v. 16), dwelling in the love of God (1. John iv. 16), abiding in Christ (1. John iii. 24, R.V.), walking with God (Heb. xi. 5), and Christ living in us (Eph. iii. 17).

A speaker at a convention for the deepening of the Spiritual life, said :

"Let me tell you of a man whom I know well. After an attack of influenza he became deaf in one ear, and he was recommended to go to an aurist, a specialist.

The aurist made a very careful examination, and then told him what was the reason of his deafness, and suggested a remedy. ' You are deaf in that ear, and the probability is that you will soon be deaf in the other ear also. Therefore, I suggest that you allow me to bore a hole in the drum of your ear.' He thanked the aurist for the information, but declined to comply with the suggestion. That man met a lady who had had influenza about seven times, but had found a remedy that exactly suited her and restored her to health and strength. She told him of that remedy, and he immediately procured it, and took it. Then each day he used to put his watch to his ear and listen; but for several days he could not hear it tick. At the end of ten days, however, he began to hear, and in a very short time he could hear perfectly, and hears perfectly to-day. I mention that incident just to show that the man was restored not by merely treating the symptom, but by going down to the cause of it. He was in a low physical condition, and the remedy that he took restored him to his normal condition, and then the evil was removed."

So it is spiritually, unless we deal with the root of the evil there will be no adjustment; which means, no power, no communion, no victory, and no blessing in the abundant life of the Word.

IV. HOLINESS IS OBEDIENCE TO THE LORD.

" As children of obedience, not fashioning yourselves according to your former lusts in the time of your ignorance; but like as He which called you is holy, be ye yourselves also holy in all manner of living " (1. Pet. i. 14, 15, R.V.). The Holy Spirit bases this command to holiness upon the believer's relationship as a child of God. As obedient children we are "to be holy in all manner of living," as the Revised Version renders the word "conversation." The Gospel invitation is *to all men*, but when the Gospel is received by the individual it demands *all the man*. The grace of God which brings salvation purifies the heart of love, centralises the mind of thought, guides the feet of obedience, fixes the soul of affection, captivates the spirit of fellowship, attracts the eyes of faith, uses the hands of service, clarifies the vision of outlook, and rivets the ears of attention.

"Visibility and universality" are Popish marks of a true church, and Protestant marks of a true Christian. A hypocritical Jehu will do "some things"; a murderous Herod will do "many things"; but an upright Paul is "in all things willing to live honestly." Swinnock says: "It may be said of true sanctity, as the sun, 'there is nothing hid from the heat thereof.' When all the parts of the body have their due nourishment distributed to them, it is the sign of a healthy temper. As the saint is described sometimes by a 'clean heart,' so also sometimes by 'clean hands,' because he has both; the holiness of his heart is seen at his fingers' ends." The willing heart of love always expresses itself in the working hands of obedience.

Obedience is the *ring* that proves the genuineness of the coin of our faith, as Samuel said to Saul, "to obey is better than sacrifice" (1. Sam. xv. 22); obedience is the *obtainer* of the Spirit's power, for He is only given to those who "obey" (Acts v. 32); obedience is the *securer* of future blessing, for Christ is the Author of

The Sanctity of the Spiritual Life.

eternal salvation to all who "obey" (Heb. v. 9); obedience is the *feature* which shows our relationship to the Lord, as is evidenced in the act of Abraham when he responded to the Lord's direction (Gen. xxii. 18; Heb. xi. 8); obedience is the pass that gives the right to enter into the place of blessing, as the Lord says, " If ye be willing and obedient, ye shall eat the good of the land " (Isa. i. 19); obedience is the *feeder* of a beneficent influence, as the apostle indicates when he says of the saints in Rome, " your obedience is come abroad unto all " (Rom. xvi. 19); obedience is the *lesson* the Lord would ever teach us, as the greatest of all teachers exemplifies—" He learned obedience by the things He suffered " (Heb. v. 8); obedience is the *credential* that evidences our fitness for service, and the *precursor* of reward, as is shown in the life of Christ: He became " obedient unto death, wherefore God highly exalted Him " (Phil. ii. 8, 9); obedience is the *mark* that evidences our love to our Lord, as he says, " If ye love Me, ye will keep My commandments " (John xiv. 23); obedience is the *sum total* of the Christian life, for there is no holiness without it; in fact, *obedience is holiness*, for we can only purify our souls by " obeying the truth " (1. Pet. i. 22).

There is no holiness apart from obedience. Obedience to the Lord is the very soul of holiness, yea, is holiness itself. When we obey we are holy. Do not think holiness means attending a religious convention, or going to an altar for a blessing; these may be the soul's expression to be right with the Lord, but obedience is the soul's response to the Lord as He speaks in the Word of His direction. As long as we are obeying Him we need not be troubled about feeling, or blessing, or power. Obedience is power, is blessing; for, being in the place of God's will, we have His blessing.

V. Holiness is the Recognition of the Lord.

The recognition of the Lord is to recognise Him *as Lord*. "Sanctify Christ as Lord in your hearts" (1. Pet. iii. 15, R.V.). These words describe faith's double action, namely, setting apart the heart to the Lord, as when a house is set apart for a particular person's occupation; and the setting apart of the Lord for the heart, as when an outgoing tenant delivers the keys up to the possession of the incoming one. He is thus recognised as in the place of authority, ownership and right. We have nothing to give to Him, for He owns everything, ourselves included.

What a difference there is between law and grace. Under the law a Jew was expected to yield a tenth of his income to the Lord; but under grace we recognise, if He is Lord, that everything belongs to Him. Hence the frequency with which the apostle uses the familiar figure when speaking of himself and his service, namely, that of a slave. The Greek word "*doulos*" does not mean one who serves for another, but one who is owned by another. He is the property of his master. Paul's attitude and action were but his faith's recognition of the teaching of Christ. Every simile he uses brings out the truth of his own words when he said, "Whose I am and Whom I serve" (Acts xxvii. 23). He is an *ambassador* as representing the authority which sends him (II. Cor. v. 20); he is a *vessel* to be used by a power outside of him (Acts ix. 15); he is a *steward* as being

The Sanctity of the Spiritual Life. 93

responsible to a master over him (I. Cor. iv. 1); he is a *channel* of blessing through which passes the supply which is conserved in the great reservoir (Col. i. 29); he is a *limb* in the body of Christ, which is moved by the will of the Great Head (I. Cor. xii. 3-14); he is the *casket* which contains the light of the treasure of God's wealth of grace (II. Cor. iv. 7); and he is the *pattern* which proclaims the skill of the Great Workman (I. Tim. i. 16).

Paul emphasises the same truth in his teaching. One sentence, like a star of the first magnitude, shines out in the sky of his testimony, and that is, " The Lord." When it is a case of discipline in judging the erring brother at the church at Corinth, the church is to gather " in the name of the Lord Jesus " (I. Cor. v. 4), that they may act in kindly faithfulness and impartiality, and yet in strict conformity with the will of God. When the apostle chides the saints at Corinth with their looseness regarding the Lord's Supper, in the unholy manner in which they were observing it, he emphasises the Lordship of Christ again and again. He reminds them of the revelation he had " received of the Lord," that " *the Lord's* supper " was to be observed, that "the cup *of the Lord*" represented " the blood of the Lord," and that if they kept the feast as He directed they did shew forth " *the Lord's* death," and if they acted in disobedience in contrary action, they were chastened by " the *Lord* " (I. Cor. xi. 20-32). Saints were commanded to " marry in *the Lord*," that is, He was to be consulted as to the one who was to be taken in marriage. Children are to obey their parents " *in the Lord*," that is, as long as the parents are acting in the authority of the Lord they are to be under their authority. Every relationship of life, according to the Epistle to the Ephesians, is to be under the supervision, at the dictation, in the presence of and with regard to the Lord as such. When He is thus sanctified as Lord in our hearts, we find being in bondage to Him is our freedom.

VI. HOLINESS IS BEING OCCUPIED BY THE HOLY ONE.

There is a great difference between religion and holiness. Some of the most religious people are the most unholy. Paganism is associated with religious rites, while it practices licentious ways. The Prophet Ezekiel describes a number of priests who were zealously occupied in the temple service, while their hearts were filled with "wicked abominations" (Ezek. viii. 8-12). Paul said to the Athenians they were "too religious" (Acts xvii. 22, R.V.); they had the altar of religious observance erected to the "unknown god," but they were utterly in the dark as to the Lord, Whom to know is life eternal. Romanism in the name of religion has done some of the most diabolical and abominable things under the sun; and some Protestants have used the cloak of a religious profession to hide the diseased nature of an unrighteous life. The corruption of paganism, the ignorance of heathenism, the hatred of Romanism, and the inconsistency of Protestantism suggest the opposite of these, namely: purity, knowledge, love, and righteousness, each of which is a correlative and an illustration of holiness.

Religion is an outward act, it may be good or bad; holiness is an inward life, which like a good vine proves itself by the fruit it bears. Religion is something put

The Sanctity of the Spiritual Life. 95

on; holiness is Someone living out. "Holiness is not Christ *and* me, but Christ *in* me." All holiness resolves itself in the Holy One. It is as the Holy One Himself comes and lives in our hearts that He reproduces the holiness of Himself in our lives. There is all the difference in the world between the sun and the moon; one is a giver of light and the other is the reflector; the one emits, and the other transmits; the one shines by its own light, and the other shines by the light of another. As the fire of the sun makes the sun what it is, so Christ dwelling in the heart makes the Christly life. When Christ was transfigured the transforming power was within. The inherent glory flashed out. Holiness is the Holy One shining through us, even as the electricity makes the wire luminous by possessing it.

Dr. Leighton Parks, of Boston, America, told the following story of a young Japanese, who came to his study one day. The maid opened the door, and the young man entered very abruptly, and said: "*Sir, can you tell me how to find the beautiful life?*" Dr. Parks answered, "Do you wish to talk to me about religion?" "No, sir; I merely want to find out about the beautiful life." "Have you ever read the Bible?" "Yes, sir; I have read some; but I don't like the Bible." "Have you ever been to church?" "Yes; I have been twice; but I don't like the church. I am trying to find the beautiful life. Many of your people do just as our Japanese people do. They are bad, they cheat and tell lies, and yet they are all Christians. That is not what I want. I do not want your religion. But there is something I want. I cannot tell what it is. I call it the beautiful life, and they told me perhaps you could tell me about it." "Where did you ever hear about it?" "I never heard about it, but I saw a man in a boarding-house in San Francisco, soon after I landed—a poor man, not an educated man, like myself. I have studied in a university in Japan, and now am studying in one of your great universities. This was a poor man, an old man, a carpenter; but he had what all my life I have wanted. I have thought it might be in the world, but I have never seen it in my own country; I call it the beautiful life. How can I find it? This old man went about helping everybody; he was always happy; he never thought about himself. I knew him three weeks, and watched him all the time, and I felt I must have what he had. I have seen some other people who have had it. I do not know what it is; it cannot be your religion, because you do not all have it."

Then Dr. Parks read him the 13th chapter of the 1. Corinthians, that beautiful love chapter, that means so much to us, and asked, "Is that it?" The Japanese said, "Yes, perhaps, it sounds like it; but how can I get it?" Then Dr. Parks told that wonderful story of the perfectly beautiful life, and tried to tell him very simply, and said, "Now you have just to follow that Life," and then, as he was obliged to go, he gave him a copy of the New Testament. The Japanese asked, "Can you not give me a more modern book?" You know the Japanese are very up-to-date. But he said, "No, it is not in any other book, although I will give you some other books that will help you; but this is the one Book you need. You may study it, and pray that light may be given you to live the beautiful life."

Dr. Parks heard nothing from the young man for a

year or two, and then received a letter, saying, "I am called back to my own country to an important position. Before I go, I must see you. May I call at a certain hour?" As he could not be at home at that hour, Dr. Parks wrote that he would see him the following day. The following day came, but the man did not appear, and he gave him up. The next day, just at noon, he burst in, as he had done before, very abruptly, saying: "My train leaves at two o'clock. I must take that train to catch the steamer at San Francisco, to go back to my own country. I have something to tell you." But he did not need to tell one word; it was all written on that radiant face. "Sir, I have found the beautiful life, I have found Jesus," he exclaimed; and then, unable to linger, he went back to his own country, to tell the people of the Life once lived here on earth, and lived here again in the lives of God's children to-day.

CHAPTER VIII.

NEED: THE DEPENDENCE OF THE SPIRITUAL LIFE.

"He is full of emptiness," said one of another, who was lacking in stability and solidity. As a scientific fact it is an impossibility to be full of emptiness, and as a spiritual experience too, for if we are not full of grace we are full of something which is the opposite. Yet emptiness is expressive of a lack, a want, the need of something to be supplied. A consciousness of need is the pre-requisite to the supply of the need; and yet there is a happy paradox, for he whose need is most met feels he needs the more. Heaven's blessings satisfy the longing soul, and make the soul long the more. The Lord filleth the hungry with good things, and the good things create an appetite which makes the hunger the more intense. We never need want when we have Christ, but we never get beyond wanting in our need of Him. The sufficiency of His grace meets us in every place, as we have a place for Him Who is the grace of our sufficiency. The emptiness of our expressed need is always met by the endowment of His loving answer. He who thinks he does not need anything has need of everything, while he whose need is met in everything knows he has nothing.

Let us ponder a few Scriptural propositions as we think of the need-expressed life.

I. GOD DISLIKES EMPTINESS.

"The whole earth is full of His glory," chanted the

Seraphs in their holy song of worship, and all nature illustrates the fact to those who have eyes to see it.

> "Earth's crammed with Heaven,
> And every common bush afire with God;
> But only he who sees, takes off his shoes—
> The rest sit round it and pluck blackberries."

A single seed-pod of a pansy has in it from fifty to a hundred seeds. For all the light and heat rays from the sun which our earth receives, six hundred million times as many are radiated away into space. In every pound of chalk there are at least shells of a million animals. God is prodigal with His supplies, and demonstrates beyond question that He abhors a vacuum. He as much dislikes emptiness in the moral and spiritual realm. When He brought Israel out of Egypt He said, " Ye shall not go empty " (Exod. iii. 21), hence He influenced the Egyptians to give them an abundant supply (Exod. iii. 22, R.V.). When Jehovah instructed His people to come to the annual feasts, He strictly enjoined them that they should not appear before Him empty (Exod. xxiii. 15; xxxiv. 20; Deut. xvi. 16); and he also commanded the master, when he liberated the slave, in the year of Jubilee, to deal with him in a liberal manner. He said, " When thou sendest him out free from thee, thou shalt not let him go away empty: thou shalt furnish him liberally out of thy flock, and out of thy floor, and out of thy wine-press " (Deut. xv. 13, 14).

The Lord dislikes emptiness, shallowness, unreality, in the worship and work of His people. " Bring no more vain [empty] oblations " is His cutting charge to Israel, when they were observing the ritual of His law and knew nothing of the reality of His grace. "Whited sepulchres," Christ called the self-righteous Pharisees, and "full of dead men's bones"—full, and yet empty of the essentiality of the life which is the "life indeed." "Poor, blind and naked," is the verdict of the Lord against the Laodicean church. The church was inflated with the wind of self-conceit and blown out with the inflatus of self-sufficiency, while it was suffering with the big-head of pride and boasted it had need of nothing. Of the prodigal son in the far country we read, "he began to be in want." The word "*want*" is the same as rendered "*come short*" and "*fail*" in Heb. iv. 1 and xii. 15. In the first Scripture we are reminded that there is a possibility of coming short of God's rest, and in the second of failing of His grace, and thus being pauperised of the very things which make efficient and sufficient in the spiritual life.

Let us remember that the Lord abominates that which is empty, vain, lacking, and not answering to His will. Pope says,

> "Empty heads console with empty sound."

Empty heads find consolation in things with which they correspond. The Lord does the opposite. He in wondrous grace corresponds to our expressed need with His satisfying love. Are we conscious of our need of His sanctifying love, His ennobling grace, His holy truth, His keeping power, His guiding Spirit, and His gladdening joy? Then let us rejoice in the fact that "God sendeth and giveth both mouth and meat," that is, He creates the need and meets it.

II. THE LORD IS OBLIGED TO EMPTY US BEFORE HE CAN FILL US.

Under the law when a house was infected with leprosy one of the first things, before the house was entered and cleansed by the priest, was to empty it (Lev. xiv. 36). The same principle holds in the lives of God's people. Naomi confessed, " I went out full but the Lord brought me home empty " (Ruth i. 21). He had to bring her to the end of her resources, and make her conscious of her own utter destitution ; then she knew the kinsman redeemer as the restorer of her life, and the nourisher for the rest of her days, and following this she became of use in nursing the child of Boaz, and thus was identified with the royal line of David, and David's greater Son.

Launcelot, in Tennyson's "Idylls of the King," stands before the master whom he has wronged, the noble Arthur, the Poet's type of the Christ, and says,

> " In me lived a sin
> So strange, of such a kind, that all of pure,
> Noble, and knightly in me twined and clung
> Round that one sin, until the wholesome flower
> And poisonous grew together, each to each,
> Not to be pluck'd asunder."

The " one sin " corrupts the " wholesome flower " till they " poisonous grew together." It is always so, the one poisonous thing poisons the non-poisonous. The blessed thing becomes a curse when contaminated by an accursed thing. This is illustrated in the history of the brazen serpent. When the Israelites looked to it in obedience to Jehovah they got life ; but when they worshipped it instead of Him then they were guilty of idolatry (II. Kings xviii. 4). There must be wholehearted response to Him if there is to be a full-hearted answer from Him. He will act for us and in us as we fulfil His direction. Everyone of His blessings is conditioned upon our obedience. The offending eye and hand have to be plucked out and cut off before there is the sense of His approving love. The heart has to be cleansed ere there is the beatific vision. The weight has to be laid aside to run the race with patience, that the prize may be obtained. Separation from the world of sin and sinners is essential to experience the indwelling and the out-working of the Almighty. The acknowledgment of the Lord in the path of obedience is pre-requisite for His guiding. The abiding with the Lord in fellowship is commanded for the Lord's answered prayer; and the utter sense of weakness and emptiness, precedes His filling and empowerment. As Flavel says: "When God intends to fill a soul, He first makes it empty; when He intends to enrich a soul, He first makes it poor; when He intends to exalt a soul, He first makes it humble; when He intends to save a soul, He first makes it sensible of its own misery, want and nothingness."

III. GOD WANTS OUR EMPTINESS FOR HIS FILLING.

Man's impotence is the condition for the display of God's omnipotence. When Gideon's three hundred men went against the Midianites, they carried empty pitchers, in which they placed lights, and the smashing of the pitchers revealed the lights, and dazzled and nonplussed their enemies (Jud. vii. 16). Paul uses this very fact, when he says, in speaking of the Gospel in its power, "We have this treasure in earthen vessels, that the excellency of the power may be of God" (II. Cor. iv. 7). When the empty pitcher of our being is possessed by the light of the Lord's presence, then there is the flashing forth of the light of His truth.

"Go borrow thee vessels . . . empty vessels" (II. Kings iv. 3), was Elisha's direction to the widow with a pot of oil; and when the vessels were procured, she poured from her limited oil an unlimited supply. Here again emptiness is met by Divine fulness. Scripture abounds with illustrations of how God meets His people in the time of their extremity. *Jacob* prevailed with the angel and became a prince with God as he clung to Him in his weakness; *Israel* at the Red Sea was hemmed in on every side, but God made a path through the waters; the *bitten, helpless Israelites* found life and health in looking to the God-provided remedy; *the stripling David* with God, in his utter weakness was more than a match for Goliath in his strength without God; *the Apostle* with the thorn in the flesh cast himself in his utter impotence upon the omnipotence of the living Christ and thus found the devil to be a means of grace; and *the beloved John* in his banishment to the Isle of Patmos found himself nearer heaven and Christ than if he had been without the persecution.

One of the most striking examples of what God can do in answer to faith and prayer was the late George Muller. What was the secret of his blessing? In a few terse words his old friend, the late Robert Chapman, of Barnstaple, gave it. He said, "I have known him intimately for sixty-eight years. We remembered each other daily at the throne of grace. If I were asked to write the biography of Brother Muller I should say *he brought everything to God*, small and great, temporal and eternal, and *he brought God into everything*. The details are written above, and to-morrow morning we shall have leisure to read them. The night is far spent and the day is at hand." Robert Chapman gives us the secret of the spirituality of Muller's life, in two brief sentences: "He brought everything to God, and he brought God into everything." The simplicity of his life is expressed in bringing everything to God, and the sanctity of his life in bringing God into everything. A whole treatise might be written on the subject of sanctification, but no treatise could express more than bringing God into everything and everything to God.

IV. WHAT ARE THE CONDITIONS TO THE FILLING OF THE SPIRIT?

As there were steps to the throne of Solomon before he got into the seventh place of the seat, so there are seven steps to take, conditions to fill, before the Spirit in His fulness is possessed and His fulness maintained. *We emphasise "maintained," because so many who obtain Him in His presence do not retain Him in His power.* The conditions may be summed up under the following seven words, confession, application, sanctification, resignation, appropriation, recognition, and transmission.

1. *Confession.* "I went out full, and the Lord hath brought me home again empty" (Ruth i. 21), is the confession of Naomi as she relates her wandering from the Lord, and her restoration to Him. "Call me not Naomi, for that means pleasant, hence I am wrongly

named; but call me Mara, which signifies bitterness, for that is more fitting to my self-experience." She had brought bitterness to herself by her restless wandering, and the bitterness had driven her back to the Lord in heart-confession and need.

Confession is heart-revealing. It is the bringing out into the light of the Lord's presence the sin which led away from Him, as Joseph's brethren did, when they owned the wrong they had done to their brother. *Confession is sin-condemning.* It is not being sorry for the consequence of the wrong done merely, it is hating the wrong because it is wrong and condemning it, as Israel did, when they stoned Achan to death. *Confession is iniquity-naming.* It is more than asking for forgiveness, it is the naming to the Lord in detail the iniquity which caused us to err, as Achan did, when he said, " I saw a goodly Babylonish garment, and two hundred shekels of silver, and a wedge of gold of fifty shekels, and I took them " (Josh. vii. 21). *Confession is soul-humbling.* The contrite and humble spirit, and the broken heart are expressed conditions of the being which are well-pleasing to the Lord, and not the glib tongue of mere expression. The waxing old of the bones which expresses the deep consciousness of felt anguish on account of sin, leads to permanent soul-blessing. *Confession is sin-killing.* It does not compromise with sin, nor parley with it, as King Saul did with the Amalekites, but it hews it in pieces as Samuel did Agag. *Confession is need-announcing.* When we confess we have no might, then we are in a position to know the meaning and blessedness of the Lord's promise, " that to them who have no might He increaseth strength " (II. Chron. xx. 12;

Isa. xl. 29). And *confession is blessing-bringing*. When Gideon confessed that he was " poor " and the " least " in his father's house, the Lord promised to be with him in victory, and the Spirit clothed Himself with him (Judges vi. 12-16, 34, R.V.). In a word, confession puts us in touch with the Lord, and that touch brings the power into us from Him which makes us efficient in every way.

2. *Application*. The Lord does not, as a rule, give His blessings without being asked for them, but no one ever asked His blessing without getting it. Heaven's emptied-out blessings come to those who bring the tithes of the Lord's requirement to Him (Mal. ii. 10, R.V.). *Cleansing* came to the leper who said to the Lord, " Thou canst make me clean." *Sight* came to the blind man who sought the mercy of the Son of David. Sinking Peter was *saved* in response to his " Lord, save me." Zaccheus sought to see the Saviour, and the Saviour sought and saved the man who sought to see Him; the Syro-phenician woman appealed to the Lord to deliver her daughter, and she got all she asked, and more; and the disciples asked the Christ to explain His teaching to them, and He responded, and revealed to them the mysteries of the Kingdom. The same thing holds good with reference to the Spirit, Christ assures us : " If ye then, being evil, know how to give good gifts to your children, how much more shall your heavenly Father give the Holy Spirit to them that ask Him " (Luke xi. 13). There is a sense in which we do not need to ask for the Spirit. We do not need to ask Him to *come to us ;* but there is a sense in which we do need to ask Him to *come in* and take full possession. We

do not need to ask the sun to *shine on* to the window, but it will not *shine into* the room if the shutters are closed. One relates how he came on one occasion to a gate in Scotland. The gate-keeper's daughter ran down to the gate and closed it, saying as she did so, " You have not to pay anything for passing through this gate ; all you have to say is, ' Please, allow me to pass through.' " The young man did as he was told, and immediately he was allowed to pass through the gate. The owner maintained the right of way by stipulating the condition, and yet everyone had the right of way who asked. The same holds with reference to the Spirit. They who seek the blessing of His empowering presence, shall never want the blessing of His power. Application to the Lord will surely bring a hearty response from Him.

3. *Separation*. " The emptiers have emptied them out " (Nahum ii. 2), is what Jehovah said Israel's enemies had done to His people. We may apply the words to ourselves. We turn emptiers that we may empty out everything displeasing to the Lord. The " put away " of evil in obedience to the Lord's command always precedes the Lord's promise, " I will purge away thy dross, and take away all thy sin " (Isa. i. 16, 25). " Shake thyself from the dust " must be obeyed before the Lord can say, " How beautiful are the feet of him that bringeth good tidings " (Isa. lii. 2, 7). The Egypt of the world must be forsaken, before we can have communion with the Lord at Bethel, as Abraham (Gen. xiii. 3, 4). Obeyed commands always command the promises to be fulfilled. As we obey the " come out " of separation from the unclean thing of the world, we experience His promise of power, " I will dwell in you and will walk in

you" (II. Cor. vi. 15-18). There is no royal road to the full possession of the Spirit, other than obedience (Acts v. 32).

4. *Resignation.* To resign, not only means to give up, but to assign back. Both thoughts may be embodied as we think of submission to the Lord and the recognition of His absolute claim over us. The spirit of such a resignation is aptly illustrated in David's mighty men, who not only submitted to his authority, but said, "Thine are we, David, and on thy side," and thus owned his claim (I. Chron. xii. 16-18). As we yielded our will to the Lord in our conversion when we abandoned our own thoughts, so in consecration we yield our whole being to Him to be dominated by Him. A working man in speaking of his conversion said, "I just chucked myself into the arms of Jesus, the same as when I had my arm amputated, I told the surgeon, 'I am in your hands, you must do with me just what you think best.'" When we leave ourselves in the hands of the Lord for Him to do as He thinks best, He always does the best. The way to secure the best, is to give ourselves over to the Best One.

5. *Appropriation.* The next thing to our giving, is to believe that the Lord takes. One has well said, in referring to the faith of a Christian, "It is the faith of a transaction; it is not the committing of one's thought in assent to a proposition, but it is the trusting of one's being to Another Being, there to be rested, kept, guided, moulded, governed, and possessed forever."

We hold Him because He holds us, as the needle clings to the magnet because the magnet holds the needle. We take Him to undertake for us, as the friend assumes the responsibility for another when he undertakes all the arrangements of a journey. We should not be concerned about our holding or taking, for we shall get into bondage if we do, but we should recognize that He has undertaken, and rest and be content.

"Do you think my faith will hold out?" asked a believer of her minister. "Well, I don't know much about your faith, but I am sure Jesus Christ will hold out, and that's enough for you. Look not at your faith, but unto Him."

6. *Recognition.* When the prophet Zechariah had the vision of the golden lampstand and the two olive trees, which fed the light with their oil, he asked, "What be these two olive branches, which through the two golden pipes empty out of themselves oil into the gold?" (Zech. iv. 12, margin). He is told they represent two anointed ones. The marginal reading is specially suggestive, the golden pipes are said to "empty out of themselves oil into the gold." Without noting the prophetic application of these words, we may take these two anointed ones to illustrate the anointed ones mentioned in Eph. iii. 16, etc., namely, the Holy Spirit and Christ. The strengthening work of the Spirit is that the Christ (The Anointed One) may dwell in our hearts. It is as the ballast of the Spirit's presence sinks us into the fulness of the Christ that we know the fulness of God. The early mystics spoke often of practising the presence of the Lord. They recognised His presence, hence they realised its power. "I have been trying to realise the Lord's indwelling presence for years, but I see the mistake I have been making, I should have done as you said, recognise His presence and

thus realise it," said one to the writer. Many are making the same mistake; they want to realise before they recognise. But whether you realise or not, ever recognise. Those who have thus learned to recognise the Lord's indwelling presence by faith, need have no fear for their comfort, nor be concerned about their spiritual experience.

7. *Transmission.* A little girl reading about the widow with her two mites, made a mistake and read, " two mitts "; and accordingly set to work to make two mitts to give to the Lord's work. There are four words which end with " *mit,*" which we may well lay to heart, and they are—Admit, Submit, Commit, and Transmit. First, we *admit* His command to obey it; second, we *submit* to His rule, and are governed by it; third, we *commit* by prayer and faith all our concerns into His hands for His keeping; and, fourth, we *transmit* what He has given us to others. When Ruth was lying at the feet of Boaz, she got six measures of corn (Ruth iii. 17). Our Divine Kinsman Redeemer has given to us six measures of corn in the Gospel, with which to feed the poor, hungry multitude of the world, and these are: Forgiveness of Sins; Peace with God; Justification; Eternal Life; Liberty; Holiness.

All these blessings have been procured for us by means of the blood of Christ's atonement, and are made effectual by the Holy Spirit's working. The world is hungry for this Gospel, and is waiting for believers to take it to them. " The Church wants to do a little walking in the mud in the quest of lost souls," said one who had been influenced to attend a Gospel service through an open-air procession. If we want the unsaved to come to us and our Lord, we must go out of our way to reach them. And the best way to keep ourselves in the way is to go out of our way to reach the unsaved. We conserve our own blessing by giving it away to others.

> "Freely ye have received, so give,
>   Bade He Who hath given us all.
> How shall the soul in us longer live,
>   Deaf to their starving call—
> For whom the blood of the Lord was shed,
> And His body broken to give them bread,
> If we eat our morsel alone?"

CHAPTER IX.

DEPTH: THE INNESS OF THE SPIRITUAL LIFE.

"For this cause I bow my knees unto the Father of our Lord Jesus Christ, of Whom the whole family in heaven and earth is named, that He would grant you, according to the riches of His glory, to be strengthened with might by His Spirit in the inner man; that Christ may dwell in your hearts by faith; that ye, being rooted and grounded in love, may be able to comprehend with all saints what is the breadth, and length, and depth, and height; and to know the love of Christ, which passeth knowledge, that ye might be filled with all the fulness of God. Now unto Him that is able to do exceeding abundantly above all that we ask or think, according to the power that worketh in us, unto Him be glory in the Church by Christ Jesus throughout all ages, world without end. Amen" (Eph. iii. 14-21).

This prayer gives us the man of prayer on bended knees, pleading in the innermost recesses of his heart—in the holiest of all—on behalf of the inner life of the Church. Mark the frequent play upon the inness of things.

" The whole family *in* heaven and earth."

" Strengthened with might by His Spirit *in* the *inner* man."

" That Christ may dwell *in* your hearts."

" Rooted and grounded *in* love."

" Filled *into* all the fulness of God."

" According to the power that worketh *in* us."

" Unto Him be glory *in* the Church."

These mountain peaks of the Bernese Oberland of Scripture, with their snow-capped glory of Divine beauty, suggest something of the resources for the inner life of the Church.

First, *The grace of God is the cause, the centre, and the circumference of the inner life of the Church.* The family of God in heaven and earth is named, has a name, because of the Father, Who has given each member being and well-being. He Who has caused us to be, must be to us all we need in His cause. He Who has placed us in the cradle of His home, must feed us from the larder of His grace.

"That He would grant you." The Spirit had spoken of the grace which purposed in its love to have us, the grace which according to its riches has blessed us, the grace which in its glory has graced us, the grace which in its life has saved us, the grace which in its outlook will display its kindness through us, the grace which qualified the apostle to make Christ known to others, and now grace is to bestow all the essential qualifications which will make the inner life pure and complete. The word "*grant*" means to "*give freely*," and is the word which is employed to describe the gracious acts of God's grace.

Grace, the coloured man said, was: "Receiving everything for nothing, when we don't deserve anything." When we bottom our blessings and experiences on the grace of God we are on a rock foundation, and at the fount of an inexhaustible supply. When we are open to God's givings there is no lack of godliness. To be efficient in the Christian life we need to know our in-sufficiency and God's all-sufficiency. It is God's sufficiency which makes holy saints, able ministers, and victorious believers. Our God does not find fault with us because we are not better, but because we do not receive more from Him. Grace is the salt to season the speech, the oil to lubricate the soul, the health to invigorate the body, the light to illuminate the mind, the sun to warm the heart, the health to beautify the countenance, the dress to adorn the life, the fire to fuse the affection, the food to nourish the inner being, and the strength to empower the walk.

Again, *The Spirit is the power which gives ability to the inner man.*—" With power to be strengthened by means of His Spirit in the inner man." The inner man is the spirit nature. Man in the complexity of his being is composed of three departments. There is the outer court of the sense-consciousness of his body, the holy place of the life-consciousness of his soul, and the holiest of all of the self-consciousness of his spirit. The spirit as summing up the individual and intellectual life of the natural man is dead, Godward, but when man receives spiritual life he is made alive unto God; hence the inner man of the spirit is more than self-consciousness in the believer, it is God-consciousness. The Spirit comes into the inner man to make every part of the inner being fully alive unto God. Man can only answer to God, as God answers to Himself in man. He asks us to be and do, that He may be and do for us.

The Church to-day is being blighted by two evils. The one an exterior and the other an interior one. The pendulum is swinging to extremes on both sides. There is the sensuous life associated with the external attempt to please men into the kingdom of grace; and there is the sensuous life which is expressed in emotionalism, in so-called pentecostal experiences, and mere soulishness. Both of these are nothing more than religious animalism. When anyone lives in the sphere of his soul's emotionalism, instead of in the realm of his spirit in fellowship with the Spirit of God, he is dependent upon the environment of external conditions; and the consequence is, when the conditions are not favourable, he is despondent and depressed. But let the spirit touch God the Spirit, and he has an inner supply. This is happily illustrated in a Christian soldier, wounded in the Boer War, who had every particle of feeling taken from him. He was completely paralysed. The only sense he had left was sight. A friend by signs was able to converse with him. He was asked one day if God was real to him. When it is known he never slept, his answer is the more remarkable. He replied to the question, " I have twenty-four hours of sweet fellowship with God every day." Such faith in God is only possible as the Spirit of faith, yea, the very faith of Christ Himself operates in the inner man.

Archbishop Fenelon, in a letter to Madame Guyon, who had been writing to him on the possibility and power of a non-sensuous life, sought to show he had apprehended her meaning in the letter he sent her. He said, " I understand you to mean :—

" First. The subjection of the natural appetites and propensities by the grace of God through faith.

" Second. When we lose our inward sensibility, we are very apt to think we lose God, not considering that the moral life of the soul does not consist in pleasure but in union with God's will.

"Third. Entire crucifixion to any reliance upon virtues whether outward or inward. Ceasing from what God makes us and resting in Him alone.

"Fourth. Acquiescence in the will of God in trying providences. The blows which God sends upon us are received without the opposition which once existed.

"Fifth. A new life of love in God Himself, and finding in Him all the blessings of His grace.

"Sixth. A life of flexibility in God Himself. It is not enough to be merely passive under God's dealings. The spirit of entire submission is a great grace, but it is a still higher attainment to be flexible, that is, to move just as He would have us move."

Again, *The Spirit empowers the inner man that Christ may dwell in our hearts by faith.* The person who is to dwell in the heart is Christ as the Christ. As there is a progressive revelation of God in the Old Testament, so there is a progressive revelation in the New Testament of the Christship of Jesus. Christ in the gospels is a title which designates His Messiahship. He is the Anointed One to do a definite work, that work which culminated in His atoning and vicarious sacrifice on the cross.

THE TITLE, "Christ," in the Acts, becomes a proper name; hence, Peter, in speaking of Jesus as such on the day of Pentecost, says: "God hath made that same Jesus both Lord and Christ." Lord, as in the place of authority; and Christ, as the channel of blessing; hence Christ as the Christ is the Anointer to qualify others to do the work of evangelization. It is of peculiar interest to observe in the Acts that the pith of all the preaching is that "Jesus is the Christ." In the Epistles we get a further revelation of Christ as the Christ. First, in a mystical sense. Christ includes the members of the Church in their identification with the Head, and the identification of the Head with the members. The one is the completion of the other, hence Christ is the Church's fulness, and the Church is the fulness of Him Who filleth all in all. Second, Believers are said to be "in Christ," not in Jesus,—the Man Who lived on earth,—but in Christ the exalted One at God's right hand; therefore, as Lady Powerscourt said, "A Christian is not a man on earth, looking up to heaven, but a man in heaven looking down on earth." There is yet another setting of the Christship, namely, Christ in the believer. "I live, yet not I, but Christ liveth in me." "Christ in you the hope of glory." The Christian life is not the Christian imitating Christ, but Christ in the life imitating Himself. Holiness is not Christ *and* me, but Christ *in* me. Any life apart from the indwelling Christ results in self-righteousness and self-holiness. The perfect copy of Christ's life can only be reproduced by Christ Himself. We need the Copier to write the copy. We require the imitating Christ to imitate Christ. We need the Anointer for the anointing, the Blesser for the blessing, the Holy One for the holy life, the loving Christ for the compassionate heart, the Patient One for the patience of Christ, the Graced One for the graciousness of Christ, the Powerful One for the power of Christ, the Joyful One for the joy of Christ, the Prince of Peace for the peace of Christ, and the Man of Faith for the faith of Christ.

The place where Christ is to reside is in the heart.

The heart stands for three things. The will, the affection, and the mind. When Christ is owned as Lord by the will, we believe on Him with the heart. "Ye have Me in your heart," said the apostle to the saints at Philippi. In other words, he was in the warmth and love of their affection. "The eyes of your understanding or heart being enlightened," which means the Spirit's illumination of the mind. Thus the heart speaks of the will, the mind, and the affection. When Christ dwells in our will to will, in our affection to love, and in our mind to think, He has every part of our spiritual being. Let the Christ dwell in the individual and corporate heart of the Church and all will be in the harmony of happy accord. It is not the business of the members to control the Head, but for the members to be controlled by the Head. When this is the case the Church will recognise His gospel is to be the theme of her message, His love is to be the inspiration of her service, His Spirit is to be the might of her power, His authority is to be the guide of her actions, His prayer-life is to be the model for her following, His word is to be the basis of her methods, His truth is to be the mould of her character, His attitude towards her is to be her attitude towards her fellow believers, His glory is to be the aim of her life, and Christ Himself is to be the end of her existence.

Again, *The soil of God's love is the place in which we are to be grounded, rooted.* "Rooted and grounded in love." Grounded like a building securely, and rooted like a tree firmly. Good soil and good footage are essential for foliage and fruitage. The soil is Christ's love to us and not our love to Him. It is not without

The Inness of the Spiritual Life.

significance that the Greek word for love is said not to have been used by heathen writers. The soil is Divine in its composition and its consequence.

As we are rooted in His love we shall be able to apprehend with all saints what Christ is, for it takes all the saints to appreciate Him. "I belong to three Churches," said a good brother to me when travelling with him from Ireland. As he belonged to the Brethren, I said, "I thought you believed in only one Church. What are the Churches to which you belong?" He replied: "Holy Trinity, Christ Church, and all Saints."

As we recognise the latter we shall find the Lord.

The object of the saints' apprehension is the cube of Christ's Christship. The purpose of being rooted and grounded in love is that we may comprehend the breadth, length, depth, and height of the Christ. Not His love, but Himself as the Christ. The breadth of the Christ is expressed in every blessing being found in Him, all promises fulfilled in Him, and all treasure stored up in Him. The length of the Christ carries us on to the eternity of glory; hence, it is the Christ within Who is the hope of glory. The depth of the Christ takes us to the foundation fact of His atoning death, for it is the blood of the Christ Who in His own eternal spirit offered Himself to God for us;* and the height of the Christ lifts us to the dignity and royalty of what He is yet going to have and be, for it is God's purpose " in the

---

* Rotherham's comment on Heb. ix. 14 makes the eternal spirit to refer to Christ's human spirit, and not the Holy Spirit; hence, the reference is to the eternal benefit, in its endless projectiveness, of Christ's death.

dispensation of the fulness of times to gather together in one all things in the Christ, even in Him."

The first tells us we are in Christ, the second says we shall be with Christ, the third proclaims what we owe to Christ, and the last witnesses that we shall be like Christ.

"And to know the surpassing of the love of Christ." To know Him is to know His love. To know the surpassing love of the Christ is to know a love which grips us tenaciously in its hold, a love which graces us continuously in its beauty, a love which guides us unerringly in its lead, a love which constrains us unceasingly in its power, a love which consecrates us unselfishly in its life, a love which satisfies us wholly in its affection, a love which sustains us sweetly in its ministry, a love which sacrifices itself for us passionately in its service, a love which beautifies us perfectly in its holiness, and a love which fuses us in a common interest for others, so that Christ and the saints become as mingling flames in a holy sacrifice.

Again, *The implantation into His love is, that we may be immersed into all the fulness of God.* "That ye might be filled with all the fulness of God." The Greek preposition "*eis*," rendered "with," is better translated "into." We cannot contain the fulness of God, but we can be filled into it. A tumbler cannot hold the fulness that is in a full ewer of water, but it can be dropped into it, then the glass is not only filled with the water, but surrounded by the fulness that is in the jug. Knowing the love of Christ we find the fulness of God. There is a fulness of love to inspire us, a fulness of power to equip us, a fulness of grace to strengthen us, a fulness of peace to quieten us, a fulness of life to quicken us, a fulness of joy to gladden us, and a fulness of fulness to satisfy us.

Again, *The measure of God's working for us and through us is limited and guaged by His working in us.* " Now unto Him that is able to do exceeding abundantly above all that we ask or think, according to the power that worketh in us."

The pith and point of this wonderful prayer is to be found in the preposition " *kata,*" rendered " according to." " According to the riches of His glory " He ministers to us His grace and blessing, and " according to His working in us " is the condition of answered prayer. " *Kata* " with the accusative suggests an object bending towards another in order to meet its need. When we fill to the full the condition of His blessing, He fills us to the full with the blessing He has promised. The human side of the prayer life of the Church is met by the Divine side of God's ability and working. We ask much and think more, but He does more and thinks greater. The privilege of prayer is found in the " ask " of petition; the inness of prayer is suggested by the " think " of desire; the largeness of prayer is found in the " all we ask or think " of comprehensive pleading; the supply of prayer is discovered in the " abundantly " of God's munificence; the overflow to prayer is revealed in the " exceeding abundantly " of the super-abundance which goes beyond the super-abundance of the super-abundance of God's giving; the encouragement of prayer is revealed in the " God is able " of the El Shaddai of Jehovah's sufficiency; the inspiration to prayer is experienced in the " according to the power that worketh in us " of Divine inbreathing and operation; and the limitation to prayer is suggested by the "working in us," for unless we answer to Him, how can He in us answer to Himself.

This word, "exceeding abundantly above," is one of the most remarkable of Holy Writ. The word "*abundantly*" means to superabound. It is rendered "*more abundant,*" "*over much,*" and "*beyond measure.*" Then the word "*exceeding*" denotes that which is in excess of that which is over-much; then the word "above" speaks of a further excess, which is beyond the excess of the excess. Freely we might translate,— He is able to do over-much, yea, He is able to do over-over-much beyond the over-much; yea, He is able to do over-much beyond an over-over-much, beyond an over-over-over-much. This is not all, for the passage is elliptical. There is something wanting which suggests,— He is able to do over-much beyond an over-over-much; yea, beyond an over-over-over-much; yea, beyond an over-over-over-over-much.

When the Church rises to the possibility of prayer she will know the working of God's power.

"One of the greatest hindrances to Effectual Prayer is the practical listlessness and indifference with which we approach the Holiest of all, and which makes such holding on to God impossible."

"Prayer," says Dr. A. F. Schauffler, "is either a prodigious force or a disgraceful farce. If a farce, you may pray much and get little; if a force, you may pray little and get much." "If," said a plain, blunt farmer, in referring to a minister's prayer, "any son of mine should ask a favour as tamely as that minister spoke to his 'Father in heaven,' I should give him the stick."

Oh, that we might realise to the full :

> "Prayer is the mightiest force that men can wield ;
> A power to which omnipotence doth yield ;
> A privilege unparalleled,—a way
> Whereby the Almighty Father can display
> His interest in His children's need and care.
>
> "Jehovah's storehouse is unlocked by prayer,
> And faith doth turn the key. O ! would that men
> Made full proof of this wondrous means, for then
> Would mightier blessings on the Church be showered,
> Her witness owned, her ministers empowered,
> And souls ingathered ; then the gospel's sound
> Would soon be heard to earth's remotest bound.
>
> "All things are possible if men but pray ;
> And, if God did but limit to a day
> The time when He would note the upward glance,
> Or fix the place and name the circumstance,—
> When, where, or why petitions could be brought,—
> Methinks His presence would by all be sought.
>
> "But since He heareth prayer at any time,
> For any thing, in any place or clime,
> Men lightly value Heaven's choicest gift
> And all too seldom do their souls uplift
> In earnest pleading at the throne of grace.
>
> "O let us then more often seek His face
> With grateful hearts, remembering while there
> To thank our Father that He heareth prayer."

"The power that worketh in us" is the secret of all that needs to be adjusted. The power of the Holy Spirit was what the apostle ever recognized. We ever hear the throb of that power in the utterance and life of Paul. Listen, "The *operation* of God "—" *Working* which *worketh in* me mightily "—" God which *worketh* all in all "—" He Who *wrought effectually* in Peter, the

same was *mighty in* me "—" God which *worketh* in you "
—" which *effectually worketh in*" (Col. ii. 12; i. 29;
I. Cor. xii. 6, 11; Gal. ii. 8; Phil. ii. 13; I. Thess. ii. 13).
The word means not merely activity, but efficiency. It
occurs seven times in Ephesians, and it is used in
speaking " of God Who *worketh*" all things after the
counsel of His will, of *the* " *working* " of His power
which He " *wrought* " in Christ in raising Him from the
dead; the word is used of Satan's dominance over the
children of disobedience in whom he " *worketh* "; the
word describes the " *effectual working* of the Spirit in
Paul's ministry; and the " *effectual working* " of Christ
through the members of His body; and now the
apostle uses the same word in speaking of the " power
that worketh in us " (Eph. i. 11, 19, 20; ii. 2; iii. 7;
iv. 16; iii. 20). In each case the word is effectually
worketh. Something is accomplished. The Spirit alone
is the effective and sufficient Worker. His working
means the displacement of self and the enthronement of
Christ. His working separates from the world and to
fellowship with God. His working overturns the conception of carnal reason, and drives triumphantly the
chariot of truth. His working expels the fleshly and the
unclean, and ennobles the heart with holiness and purity.
His working rides down all envies and all jealousies, and
works in holy love and compassionate sympathy. His
working develops the graces of Christly character and
beautifies the life with Christly graces. His working
makes the absent Christ a present reality and makes
Him live His own life over again. His working causes
the held hands of intercession to be lifted in fervent
petition, and causes the helping hands of compassionate

help to lift the fallen to Christ's feet. His working will not only bring glory to God in the Church in the ages to come, but in this present age.

"Unto Him be glory in the Church." A good deal we have said relates to the individual life of the believer, but after all, the corporate life of the Church is dependent upon the individual life of the believer. Let each believer be adjusted to Christ, and all the believers will be adjusted to each other. When Christ as Lord dominates *the official life* of the Church, the glory of His government will be brought to God, in the officers caring for the flock as He desires, and in the flock obeying those who have the rule over them. When Christ in His life throbs through *the heart life* of the Church, the glory of His identification with the Church will be accorded to God, in the concentrated and consecrated aim of its members to conserve all things in His interests. When Christ acts in *the social life* of the Church, the glory of His holiness will be given to God, in the keeping out of its life the worldly and selfish, and in living a life of gracious concern and love in helping the weak, the poor and needy. When Christ as the Intercessor pleads in *the prayer-life* of the Church, the glory of His constant intercession and bestowments will be rendered to God, in the holy passion of the Church's agonized petition and the living record of His constant supplies and replies. When Christ in the passion and sacrifice of His cross impresses Himself upon *the giving life* of the Church, the glory of His loving and giving will ascend to God, in the correspondence of the sons of God to the Son of God in His bleeding to bless and in His sacrifice to save. When Christ in His resurrection power operates in *the spirit life* of the Church, the glory of His mighty achievements will ascend to God in the proclamation of His ability in its members to respond to God's ideals and to fulfil His requests. When Christ as the Baptizer with the Holy Spirit is received into *the active life* of the Church, the glory of His accomplishments will be given to God in the out-working of the Spirit's operations in testimony to Christ. When Christ as the Truth thinks in *the mind life* of the Church, the glory of His word and promises accrues to God in the assurance she has in her heart and the authority she possesses in her testimony. When Christ in the constraint of His love moves in *the soul life* of the Church, the glory of His affection rises to God in the compassionate heart the Church will have for the lost and the help she will give to the needy. When Christ as the Shepherd acts in *the service life* of the Church, the glory of His care answers to God in the Church carrying the lambs in the bosom of her love and serving the sheep with the help of her attention. When Christ walks amidst *the responsible life* of the Church, the glory of His cleansing and consecration will be brought to God in the elimination of the things He has against us, and the admission of Himself into the inner life that all may be subservient to Him; and when He is known as the Christ in *the privileged life* of the Church as the Satisfier, the glory of His attraction will redound to God in the Church's rest of heart and joy in Himself.

CHAPTER X.

THE HOLY SPIRIT: THE POWER OF THE SPIRITUAL LIFE.

There is all the difference in the world between the believer possessing the Holy Spirit, and the Holy Spirit possessing the believer; even as there is a difference between a person entering the house as guest and coming in as host to take absolute control and authority. Many believers know the Spirit, if they believe His Word, as the Seal, marking them as God's property, who do not know Him as Sovereign occupying the whole being in government. In the first case, the Spirit is like a man paying a deposit on purchasing an estate; and in the other He is as one who enters upon the property and obtains possession. Christ was sealed with the Spirit at His baptism, and acknowledged as the Beloved Son; but it was afterward that it was said, "He was full of the Holy Spirit," was "led of the Spirit," "Returned in the power of the Spirit," and that He said, "The Spirit of the Lord is upon Me" (Luke iii. 22; iv. 1, 14, 18). Is there not a corresponding experience in the life of the believer? Take the Epistle to the Ephesians. In that Epistle, of believers it is said, "Having believed, ye were sealed with the Holy Spirit of promise" (Eph. i. 13, R.V.). Yet in that same letter they are exhorted to be "filled in the Spirit" (Eph. v. 18, R.V.M.).

The fact is, there are three things we must never confound, and these are: the implantation of the life of the Spirit, the indwelling of the Spirit in the life He has implanted, and the infilling of the Spirit. In the first the Spirit is the Giver and Worker; in the second the Father is the Sealer and Claimer; and in the third the Son is the Promiser and Baptiser.

Someone has designated the truth about the Holy Spirit as "the lost Gospel." It is not lost so far as the testimony about His Person and work is concerned in the Word; but alas! that it should have to be written, to a very large extent the gospel of the Holy Spirit is not known experimentally. Is this not so when the life of ascending prayer is wanting, the submission to the authority of the Word is lacking, the power of God to keep from conscious sinning is not experienced, the peace of God not known in keeping carking care from the heart, the separation from the world not followed, the witness to the Lord not given, and the Christ not dwelling in the inner being?

On the other hand, there are many believers who want to know the Holy Spirit in power, who are asking the question, "How can we know when we have Christ's baptism of the Holy Spirit?"

Before I endeavour to answer the question, let me emphasise one thing: we must distinguish the *gifts* of the Spirit from the *Gift* of the Spirit. Many are working for *them* instead of *Him*; and *He* is judged not to be in possession when *they* are wanting.

If 1. Corinthians xii. is pondered carefully, it will be seen that there is no diversity in Him. Seven times over *He* is distinguished from what *He does* and *gives* by the expression "the same," or "the self-same Spirit." Do not confuse the gifts with the Gift, the works with the Worker, the administrations and the Administrator.

There are two ways in which we may look at any given topic. We may think of the cause producing the effect, as the four mighty lakes which make Niagara what it is; or we may ponder the effects which prove the cause, as the grapes prove the vine, the rays evidence the sun, the watch tells of the maker, the moving car proclaims the electricity, the house speaks of the builder, the creation asserts the Creator, and the fruit of the Spirit the Spirit. I intend to follow the latter course, and call attention to the following *seven things*, which prove that the possessor is possessed by the Holy Spirit, namely, a surrendered will, a clean heart, a righteous hand, a prayerful spirit, a clear eye, a sweet temper, and a Scripture-guided testimony.

I. A SURRENDERED WILL.

"No man can say, Jesus is Lord, but in the Holy Spirit" (1. Cor. xii. 3, R.V.). Practically these words mean that no one can recognise the Lordship of Christ but by the Holy Spirit. The testimony of the Holy Spirit to Christ is that He is Lord; i.e., He is absolute Sovereign. He claims all because He owns all. We own His claim when we let Him claim His own. All authority is given to Christ, hence the Spirit-filled man has no authority but His authority. All power is His, therefore the believer has no power but His.

What does a surrendered will mean? At least three things: a giving up, a giving over, and a leaving alone. Christ, as in everything else, is the great example. In the hour of His greatest agony He gave up His own will. His prayer was, "Not My will, but Thine be done." His life was a continuous giving over of Himself to the will of God; as He Himself expresses it, "My meat is to do the will of Him Who sent Me"; and He never took Himself out of the will of God for He ever said, "I delight to do Thy will, O My God."

A surrendered will means the giving up of our will. Christ's claim upon those who would be His disciples is, "If any man will come after Me, let him deny himself" (Matt. xvi. 24). This denial is more than denying self certain things, it is the denial of self itself.

The same word is used by all the evangelists in calling attention to Christ's being denied by Peter. "I do not know the Man," was his emphatic and sorry avowal (Matt. xxvi. 72). He turned his back upon his Lord and would not own Him. That is what the denial of self means, namely, a non-recognition of its existence—just as a person is ignored when you do not give him any recognition on meeting him in the street. Let self be denied in this way, and at once it will be apprehended that there can be no self-will, for there is no self to will. This is only possible as we see that self is crucified with Christ. The cross ends all that is associated with self. The flesh of evil is ended, the old man of habit is put off, the law of sin is broken, and the self is crucified.

All this as a matter of *account* (which God puts to our credit) is true to the believer, the one thing now is to make it *count*, that is, let what is *fact* in Christ for us, be a *factor* by Christ in us in our daily experience. A great many believe in self-crucifixion, who know nothing of the crucifixion of self. In the former it is self-endeavouring to put itself to death; but in the latter it is another putting self to death.

As the late A. J. Gordon said, "As high as the heaven

is above the earth, so far is the distance from self-crucifixion to crucifixion in Christ."

A surrendered will means the giving over of the body to the Lord. The voice of the Holy Spirit is clear and emphatic upon this point, that we are to present our bodies a living sacrifice to Him, and to yield our members as instruments of righteousness unto Him. The words " yield " and " present " in Rom. vi. 13, 19 ; xii. 1, are one and the same. It means to be present, to stand in the presence of another, to show oneself, to be near for a given purpose. Thus Gabriel is said to " stand " in the Lord's Presence (Luke i. 19), and Christ " showed " Himself to His disciples (Acts i. 3), and " stood with " Paul in the hour of his trial (II. Tim. iv. 17). It will be seen that the meaning and usage of the word suggests a definite attitude, namely, we give ourselves over to Him for the definite purpose of His use and service.

When we speak of anyone, or anything, as " given over," we mean absolutely surrendered to a specified purpose. The Word speaks of some who were given up, or over, by God to the sins they desired (Rom. i. 24, 26, 28). They loved to make their choice, and He gave them over to the choice they loved. We also read of those who, having given themselves over to lasciviousness, were past feeling (Eph. iv. 19). The opposite is true of those who have given themselves over to the Lord. They are His for His will and work, and He in turn gives Himself over to them. Surrendering to Him, and keeping in this attitude, we then find, as one has quaintly said, " We have the *beatitude* because we have the *attitude*." The beatitude of blessing always follows the attitude of consecration.

A surrendered will means leaving ourselves in God's hands. The tense of the words " present your bodies " is the aorist, which means an act once performed and a maintained attitude in consequence. The giving of ourselves once for all is to result in leaving ourselves in His hands for ever afterwards. No give and take, but give and no take back. Such a thing as *re*-consecration means that there has been desecration.

The Lord asks from us nothing less than wholehearted consecration to Himself. A little girl some time since was staying in the country with her aunt. She had a royal time : plenty of fruit, fresh butter, new-laid eggs and cream, besides the pure air, pretty flowers, and auntie's company. The time came when she had to return home. The aunt had grown fond of her niece, and the niece loved her aunt. As they sat discussing the going home to mother, the aunt said, " I don't know what I shall do without my little girl. I think I shall have to cut you in halves, and send one half to mother, and keep the other half for myself. The question comes, which half will you decide to have. Will you stay with the half that remains with me, or will you go with the half we shall send to mother ?"

The little girl sat with wondering eyes as she contemplated the situation. " Well, what are you going to do ?" said the Auntie. At last she replied, " Oh ! Auntie, I do love you, and you have been so good and kind to me, I would really like to stop with the half of me that remains with you, but I have decided that I must go with the half which is returned to mother."

The reply of the girlie illustrates what too many may want to do. They want to be half and half ; sometimes they remain in that unhappy and nauseous condition, like the Church at Laodicea, " neither hot nor cold "; but the Lord demands and commands our whole being. He will not be content with half the price. As the altar long ago had to be built of whole stones, so He asks, and asks imperatively, that our entire spirit and soul and body shall be gladly given to Him.

II. A SEPARATED HEART.

The apostolic injunction is, " Walk in the Spirit, and ye shall not fulfil the lust of the flesh " (Gal. v. 16). The flesh is here seen in direct antagonism to the Spirit. The flesh, like all sin, is a many-sided monster. Its works are seventeen in number, and group themselves into four distinct groups. There are the *sins of sensuality*, such as adultery, fornication, uncleanness, and lasciviousness; there are the *sins of superstition*, such as idolatry and witchcraft; there are the *sins of malice and social disorder*, such as hatred, variance, emulations, wrath, strife, seditions, heresies, envyings, and murders; and there are the *sins of personal excess*, such as drunkenness and revellings.

In contrast to the above there is the " fruit of the Spirit," which divides itself into three sections, like three luscious bunches of grapes on one branch of a vine; and each of these three again divides itself into three aspects, like three strings in a bunch. The first three lead our thought *Godward*, namely, love, joy, and peace, for they all come from Him, and are found only in Him. His love is the cause of our love, His joy is the soul of our gladness, and His peace is the secret of our quietness. The second three direct our minds *manward*, for they express what the believer's conduct should be towards others. Long-suffering is suffering long without being impatient; gentleness expresses itself in a manner which does not irritate, but calms and soothes; and goodness is serving others for love's sake. The last three traits of the Spirit's fruit are *personal*: faith is the personal reliance of the believer in the Lord; meekness is the personal characteristic towards Him in all His ways; and temperance is being under the Lord's control, so that all the being is completely mastered by Him.

From what we have written it will be seen that a separated heart means two things: a separation from the flesh and its works, and a separation to the Spirit and His fruit. The question arises, "How are we to clear out the works of the flesh?" There is only one way, and that is to die out to the flesh which works. How can this be done? By self-effort? No, for that is unholy self in its fancied holiness. By self-suppression? No, for that is humble self in its pride. By self-expulsion? No, for that is proud self in its humility. By self-crucifixion? No, for that is religious self in its conceit. There is only one way, as we have already stated, and that is by crucifixion with Christ.

Two students, who were seeking to know the meaning of the deeper life, went to their Professor and asked him to explain what crucifixion with Christ meant, in a practical sense. They understood that, in a positional sense, it meant they had died for their sin in Him; but they wanted to know the deeper meaning.

The Professor replied to their question somewhat as follows: "You remember So-and-So?" mentioning a former student who had died a short time before. "Yes," was the reply. "Well, go to his grave and say all the unkind things you can think of to him."

They did as they were told, wondering what the intent of it was. They came back to their teacher, and told him they had done as he wished.

"What did he say?"

"Nothing," was the reply. "How could he say anything, he is dead."

"Now," said the Professor, "I want you to go to his grave again, and say all the flattering things you can, everything that would tend to puff him up and make him proud."

They did as they were told.

"What did he say?" was the question again put to them.

"Nothing, how could he say anything, he is dead."

Then the teacher replied, "You came to me and asked me what death with Christ meant in a practical sense. It means, as there was no response to your abuse and flattery from our dead friend as you stood over his grave, so as you make Christ's death a living reality by your personal faith in Him, there is no response to the flesh from you."

Negatively, the deeper life means, a separation from the flesh, the old man and self, in the death of Christ; and, *positively*, it signifies the Christ in the Spirit known in the heart as such. Christ means the *Anointed*, and, as such, He was anointed with the Holy Spirit, and was all He was and did because of Him (Acts x. 38). He is now the *Anointer*, the One Who empowers; and it is the work of the Holy Spirit to make Him known in us as such (Eph. iii. 16, 17). When He is thus known in power, it is no longer a question of our inability, but His ability; then we shall know that His ability enables us to respond with agility and ability to all He commands and desires.

III. A RIGHTEOUS HAND.

The Apostle Paul, as he was in the consciousness of the Lord's presence, could say of his life and service, "my conscience bearing me witness in the Holy Ghost" (Rom. ix. 1). These words, in their primary application, have reference to his concern about his brethren, but they may be taken as the key-note of his life. His conscience was one which was adjusted, not according to a human standard, but to a Divine one.

There are three things which God the Holy Spirit teaches us after we are saved, and these are, to live soberly, righteously, and godly in this present evil world (Titus ii. 12). "Godly," that is, like to God; "soberly," that is, completely mastered, so that the whole of the being is in hand; and "righteously," that is, right in our transactions with others. If we are thus taught there will be no taking advantage of another's ignorance, no selling one article at two prices sold under the same conditions. We shall not only do to others as we should wish them to do to us, but shall serve others as if we were serving Christ; yea, we shall serve Him in them.

A certain disciple of the higher criticism, who was a deacon in a chapel, had a calf to sell which had a bad pedigree, so much so that he could not sell it at the place where he lived. He took it to a distant town to dispose of it. A gentleman who saw it, asked if it was all right. The deacon replied, "If you only knew the record of that calf, you would not hesitate for one moment," implying that the calf was all right. The calf was bought. Afterwards the man boasted of how he had taken the buyer in. Someone remonstrated with him, and said, "How could you, a professing Christian and a deacon, take advantage of another's ignorance?" Whereupon he replied, "You straight-laced people are too particular. We who believe in the higher criticism are not so nice!" That does not say much for what is so often called "devout criticism."

Of this we are confident, that no consecrated and Spirit-filled man would or could act in such a manner. A Spirit-filled believer lives in the consciousness of the Lord's presence, acts under obligation to Him, and in the light of the Judgment-seat of Christ.

IV. A Sweet Temper.

"Your love in the Spirit" (Col. i. 8) are the commending words which Paul could use of the saints in Colosse. Where the Spirit in His love resides, the love of the Spirit will radiate and illuminate. He can no more be present and His love not be manifested, than the light of the sun can be absent in the ignited coal, for the simple reason that the burning coal is treasured sunshine. "He took all the strike-back out of me," said a lady to the writer, in describing the Spirit's infilling. There is no explosive material in dampened gunpowder, and there is no response to sin in one filled with the Spirit.

There comes to my mind the difference under provocation between two Christian workers, both naturally of a fiery temperament. The one expressed himself, "I wish I was unconverted for five minutes. I would give it to you hot and strong." The other worker, all the while he was being taunted, calmly looked up to heaven, quietly clapping his hands, and saying, "Bless the Lord! Bless the Lord!" What could they do with him? As one remarked, "What can you do with a fellow like that?"

"I would give anything if I had a sweet temper," says one. "I have tried again and again." And the result of your trying has been, you have become more sour. You need the sweetness of Christ to make you sweet. One of the most pathetic incidents at the late Mr. Spurgeon's funeral was the remark of a wee lassie, as the tears were trickling down her cheeks, and she pointed to the moving bier: "He always put two lumps of sugar in my tea!" The sweetness she received from him made his memory sweet to her. The Lord does not promise to put two lumps of sugar in our tea, but He does promise to put His sweetness in our hearts; and when He does, people will feel we are sweet, not that we are sweet, but that He is sweet and sweetens us.

V. A Prayerful Spirit.

One of the most comprehensive exhortations in the whole of the New Testament about prayer is "Praying in the Holy Ghost" (Jude 20). The ministry of prayer is one of the most important of all ministries.

There are four main causes of backsliding, and these are: worldly association, an unbelieving heart, a neglected Bible, and a prayerless closet; and, as a rule, the first three have their rise in the last. A prayerless spirit will cause the Bible to be neglected, will allow the spirit of faith to wane, and will question the requirement of the word of the Lord to be separated to Him from the world.

"She does not give the Holy Spirit a chance," said an old Christian, who was lamenting over the backsliding state of a young one; "she does not pray." How can He have His way if we do not pray? Prayer is the heart-hunger created by the Spirit, and only He Himself can meet the hunger of the heart. Prayer is the wire along which the current of the Spirit's power runs; how can we have the power of the Spirit if the prayer is wanting? Prayer is the opener of Heaven's storehouse of blessing; how, then, can we have the blessing if we lack the opening power? Pentecost was preceded by prayer, and it was maintained by the same means. Pentecostal power is obtained and maintained by personal and united prayer.

VI. A Clear Eye.

Not without significance is it said that, Stephen being full of the Holy Spirit, saw the Lord Jesus standing at the right hand of God (Acts vii. 56). A Spirit-filled believer always sees the Lord Jesus in the place of power and privilege. He makes much of Christ and nothing of himself; in fact, he does not talk about himself, for it is possible to sing—

"Oh! to be nothing, nothing," in such a way as to say plainly—

"Oh! I am something, something."

The Spirit-filled child of God does not look around, or he would be dismayed; he does not look within, or he would be disgusted; he does not look back, or he would be defeated; he does not look at others, or he would be disappointed; he does not look at his circumstances, or he would be disheartened; he does not look at his blessings, or he would be diverted; but he looks at Christ, and is delighted. The Spirit-equipped believer says, " Christ crucified for me is my Salvation; Christ risen for me is my Acceptance; Christ with me is my Fellowship; Christ in me is my Power; Christ before me is my Example; Christ behind me is my Director; and Christ beneath me is my Comfort."

VII. A Scripture-Guided Testimony.

Of the early believers it is said that they " Preached the Gospel with the Holy Ghost " (1. Pet. i. 12, R.V.). They preached what He had inspired, and He inspired them as they preached it. " The Holy Spirit," said an old Puritan, " always rides in the chariot of His Word." If we would have Him, we must keep where He is to be found. Professor Godet points out, in commenting upon the words of Christ, " The words I speak unto you are spirit and life," that the force and meaning of the words is, that the words of Christ are not merely the channel by which the Spirit communicates spiritual life, but that those words embody the Spirit Himself; therefore, if we would have *Him*, we must have *them;* and if *they* are wanting, then *He* is wanting. But they are not wanting, in the one filled with the Spirit, for He recognises that he has the authority of the Spirit in power, as he is under the word of the Spirit's authority.

Some who limit the Holy Ghost in the truth of His Word, and water down the fact of the Divine inspiration of the Scriptures, think they can take away, modify, and fritter off truth, and get spiritual blessing. The fact is if we fritter away and limit, we can not have spiritual blessing too. When Israel limited the Holy One of Israel, they limited the supply of blessing to themselves. He has much for faith, but nothing for faithless unbelief.

The practical question comes, *Are you, my reader, filled with the Holy Spirit?* If not, why not? What hinders? If you make room for Him, He will fill the room you make. If you give yourself entirely to Him, He will give Himself entirely to you.

CHAPTER XI.

THE SECOND BLESSING: OR THE DOUBLE OF THE SPIRITUAL LIFE.

The main question which naturally arises, as we think of such scriptural terms as "being baptized with the Spirit," "full of the Spirit," or the "infilling of the Spirit," is, Is there specific teaching in the Word that there is a second definite work of grace after conversion? A two-fold answer is given to the question. Some would tell us that we have received all that God has to give at conversion in receiving Christ, and others state that there is a crisis in the life as clear and definite as when we first turned to God. The first line of teaching is expressed in the following words: "A careful study of the New Testament leads us to the conclusion that every true believer is not to wait to enjoy the possession of the Holy Spirit in His fulness and power, but is entitled to believe that he already enjoys this glorious privilege and is to act accordingly." On the other hand, there are those who admit that all Christians have the Spirit, that is, they are not utterly without Him and His influence; but He does not wholly possess and fill them as the disciples were filled at Pentecost. This line of teaching is expressed in the following words: "We must recognize the fact that to have the Spirit is one thing, but to be filled with the Spirit is quite another thing. We know from what is recorded in John's Gospel that even before the ascension the Holy Ghost had actually been given to the disciples, for Christ breathed upon them the Holy Ghost, but on the day of Pentecost they were filled with Him."

From the experimental standpoint the latter teaching is undoubtedly the teaching of the New Testament, for while it is true as a matter of purpose and God's gift that " God hath blessed us with all spiritual blessings in Christ," yet no one can deny that the majority of believers do not enter into the fulness of the blessing of Christ when they are born again. There is hardly a truth in connection with the spiritual life that has not a double application. We give the following points by way of illustration, each of which has a correspondence to the rest that follow.

Christ's death with us and our death with Christ. As believing sinners, we say that Christ died in our stead, and bore our sins in His own body on the tree (I. Pet. ii. 24). Christ is our Divine Jonah, Who voluntarily threw Himself into the waters of judgment and sank beneath their awful weight, that we might find the storm of God's wrath appeased for us, and be at rest in consequence. But as we look at the cross in the light of New Testament teaching, we see that Christ not only died apart from us as our Substitute, but that in God's reckoning we have died with Him, so that in Him we have answered for our sin, and sin now has no claim upon us in any way whatever. Hence the Holy Spirit emphasizes the fact, that sin is not only answered for in a penal sense, but that it has no right over us now, and that we are to reckon ourselves dead to its claim and to all its calls (Rom. vi. 11).

Peace with God and the peace of God. Peace with God depends upon Him, Who made peace by the blood of His cross (Col. i. 20). And we receive the benefit of peace with God through our personal faith in Christ (Rom. v. 1); but the peace of God is only enjoyed by those who are " anxious for nothing, prayerful in everything, and thankful for anything." As God's people fulfil these conditions, God fulfils His promise in causing His peace to keep their hearts and minds in Christ Jesus (Phil. iv. 7).

Salvation and Holiness. The grace of God brings us into the ark of God's salvation to our safety, and we are assured in the Word that we are safe as Christ is, for we are not only saved by grace but made to sit with Him in heavenly places (Eph. ii. 6). But holiness is separation to the Holy One, that He in His holiness may come and dwell in us in order that He may reproduce the holiness of His character in our lives. He not only tells us to come out and be separated from every unclean thing, but to be perfecting holiness in the fear of the Lord (II. Cor. vi. 14-17; vii. 1). The former is the negative side of holiness, and the latter is the positive side. Both these aspects of holiness are only possible as the Holy One lives in us. God not only saved Israel on the night of the Passover by the blood of the paschal lamb, but He also charged Israel to make a tabernacle that He might dwell among them. The same holds good in the experience of the child of God. We are saved from wrath by the blood of the Lamb, that the Lord may be sanctified in our hearts in His sovereign sway (I. Pet. iii. 15, R.V.).

Forgiveness and cleansing. Forgiveness is God's act

of mercy, whereby He blots out the past by means of the blood of Christ and sets us free from the power of sin, which once held us, for the word forgiveness means more than pardon (the word pardon never occurs in the New Testament) [Eph. i. 7]. It signifies being freed from the power of sin which caused its guilt. Cleansing by the blood of Christ signifies the removal of the pollution of sin (1. John i. 7).

In Christ and Christ in us. The Apostle Paul expressly designates a Christian as a " man in Christ " (II. Cor. xii. 2). And he further says of himself, as to the secret of his consecrated life, " Christ liveth in me " (Gal. ii. 20). The position of the believer is that he is in Christ, in all the perfection of His work and worth, and Christ should be in the believer in all the potentiality of His beautiful character.

Life and life more abundant. Christ emphatically tells us that He came, that we not only might have life, but that we might have it more abundantly (John x. 10). Two among the number of those whom Christ healed were, a woman who was suffering from a wasting disease for twelve years, and another who was bowed down by Satan. These had life, but they could not be said to have abundant life. There are many of God's children who are weighted and wasted by spiritual disease, and the only way in which they can get deliverance is to come into living contact with the living Christ by a living faith, and then find that His livingness will course through their spiritual being to their betterment and victory.

The Spirit of adoption and the Spirit of power. The saints at Galatia had the Spirit of adoption, for the

Father had sent forth the Spirit in their hearts, crying, "Abba, Father," but they were not walking in the Spirit; hence the longing of the apostle that Christ might be formed in them that they might so walk (Gal. iv. 6-19; v. 25). It is one thing to be a child in a family, and it is quite another thing to be an obedient child.

Rest from Christ and rest with Christ. There is a two-fold rest mentioned in Matt. xi. 28, 29. The first is the rest of conscience, which Christ gives to those who respond to His invitation, "Come unto Me and I will give you rest." And the second is the rest of heart, which is found by being yoked with Him in the will of God, and thus keeping step with Him and learning of Him as He instructs us in the essential blessing of meekness.

Made meet for the inheritance and made meet for the Lord's service. Believers are exhorted to give thanks unto the Father, Who hath made them meet, or sufficient, to be partakers of the inheritance of the saints of light (Col. i. 12). This meetness is founded upon God's act of grace, and is found in Him Who is the delight of God's heart. It is independent of us, as we may readily see, as we emphasize the words, "Who hath made." The act of God's grace in making us "meet" and the tense as expressed in the "hath made," tell us of our completeness and sufficiency. The other meetness stands out in striking contrast as Paul indicates when he urges Timothy to be a vessel unto honour, sanctified and meet for the Master's (or Lord's) use (II. Tim. ii. 21). No servant is meet for the Master's use who is not sanctified and cleansed. No one would think of using a defiled vessel for ordinary use, neither will the Lord use His servants for His extraordinary work unless they are meet.

Accepted in the Beloved and acceptable to the Lord. We are made sons in the Son, saints in the Holy One, and we are beloved in the Beloved. Yea, we are much "graced," as the word accepted really means, as may be gathered from the use of the word, which only occurs in one other place (Luke i. 28), when the angel says to Mary, "Thou art much graced" (margin).

The practical outcome of being accepted in the Beloved is tersely expressed by the apostle when he says, "We make it our aim to be accepted of Him" (or well-pleasing unto Him) [II. Cor. v. 9). He is thinking of the time when he will stand before the judgment seat of Christ, when motives will be judged, and secret things brought to light; hence, meantime, he is ambitious to see to it that his motives are true, and that his life is open.

Made nigh and coming near. Believers are made nigh to God by the blood of Christ (Eph. ii. 13). And they are exhorted to draw near with a true heart and in full assurance of faith as worshippers (Heb. x. 22). To try to harmonize these two Scriptures is to find one's self in a quandary, but to remember the one refers to God's act of love in bringing us to His heart and home, and the other is His word of direction as to what He requires of us as His priests, is to see that the one is the counterpart of the other.

Union and communion. Believers are united to Christ, the Head, and to each other by the act of the Holy Spirit in baptizing them into the one body (I. Cor.

xii. 13). But to be in the unity of the Spirit is to have everything in common with the Lord, and thus to know the joy of His companionship and the helpfulness of His presence.

Sealed and filled with the Spirit. While the sealing of the Spirit may be differentiated from believing in the Lord in their order, yet they practically take place at the same time. That is, the sealing is consequent upon believing, as the Revised Version indicates in Eph. i. 13, "Having also believed, ye were sealed with the Holy Spirit of promise." But these saints at Ephesus, who were sealed, are exhorted to be filled with the Spirit. The sealing of the Spirit is the presence of the Holy Spirit in the believer, which is God's mark upon him that he is the Lord's property, while the being filled " in the Spirit " (R.V., margin), is to be surrounded by the atmosphere of the Spirit's presence, which separates us from everything that is not pleasing to the Lord, and inspires us to full obedience to the word of His direction.

Born of the Spirit and baptized with Him. We now come to the specific teaching about the Holy Spirit as it relates to the spiritual life in the holiness of its character, in the triumphs of its victories, and in the power of its service. We cannot do better in seeking to emphasize this, than to call attention to the unmistakable contrasts between being born of and baptized with the Spirit.

A Twofold Reception.

We become children of God by receiving Christ as our Saviour. "To as many as received Him, to them gave He power to become the children of God" (John i. 12). But we have the power to act as children when we know the meaning of the words of Christ—" Ye shall receive power, the Holy Spirit coming upon you " (Acts i. 8, margin). There is no doubt that the first is a definite reception which is associated with a crisis in the life, which we call conversion. Is there not equally another crisis suggested in the definite receiving of the Spirit? It is beyond all question that as a rule the anxious inquirer receives Christ only in conversion, and generally there is another crisis in the receiving of the Spirit which is the result of whole-hearted consecration.

It is of peculiar interest to trace the verb "to receive" as found in association with the Holy Spirit. Christ tells us that it is impossible for the world to receive the Spirit—" Whom the world cannot receive " (John xiv. 17). He promises to those who believe on Him that out of them shall flow rivers of living water; and this, as He intimated, refers to the Spirit Whom those who believe on Him should receive (John vii. 39). When in the upper room He said to the disciples, " Receive ye the Holy Ghost," and He promised to them that they should receive power, the Holy Spirit coming upon them.

In reading through the Acts we find those who received the Spirit, received Him in a very definite way. The believers at Samaria, who had been brought to Christ through the preaching of Philip, afterwards received the Spirit when the apostles came down to them (Acts viii. 15, 17). And when Simon Magus saw that the Spirit was conferred by the laying on of hands, he wished to obtain the same power, hence he said, " Give me also this power, that on whomsoever I lay hands, he may receive the Holy Ghost " (Acts viii. 19). The same thing took place in the house of Cornelius, for Peter, in referring to baptism, says, "They have received the Holy Ghost as well as we" (Acts x. 47). Again, the same experience is repeated in the case of the disciples at Ephesus (Acts xix. 2-6).

In three of the epistles the definite reception of the Spirit is referred to. Paul, in writing to the Church at Corinth, says, "We have received the Spirit which is of God" (1. Cor. ii. 12); and in rebuking the saints at Galatia, because they had gone back into legalism, he asks the question, "Received ye the Spirit by the works of the law or by the hearing of faith?" And he also reminds them that Christ's purpose in dying was, that they might receive the Spirit through faith (Gal. iii. 14). The beloved John, in writing to his children in the faith, reminds them of the "anointing which ye have received" (1. John ii. 27).

We recognize that in the case of the Corinthians and the Galatians they had gone back from what the reception of the Spirit meant, but the main thing is the fact that He had been received. Dr. Elder Cumming, in referring to this phrase of receiving the Spirit, says, "It is one which is specially used of the event which took place at Pentecost; that it continued to be used by the inspired writers with reference to believers since, and that there is no reason for asserting that it applies only to a case of conversion among men now, any more than it did at Pentecost among the apostles."

A Twofold Gift.

When Achsah was asked by her father, Caleb, what he should give her, she replied, "Give me springs of

The Double of the Spiritual Life.

water. And he gave her the upper springs and the nether springs" (Josh. xv. 19; Judg. i. 15). Caleb gave his daughter a double portion. And we who believe in Christ have a double portion given to us. The nether spring of the water of life, which comes from the God-given and God-smitten Rock of Ages; and the upper spring of the Spirit's inflowing grace, which is poured out by the ascended and exalted Christ as His love-gift to His saints. The Hebrew words rendered "upper" and "nether" are suggestive. "*Nether*," in its noun form means the depths, the womb, and as an adjective is often used to describe the "*lowest* hell" (Deut. xxxii. 22; Psa. lxxxvi. 13), the "*lower parts*" of the earth (Psa. lxiii. 9; Isa. xliv. 23). and is used by the psalmist in referring to God's work in forming the body in the womb when he says, "I was curiously wrought in the *lowest parts* of the earth" (Psa. cxxxix. 15). Christ went to the lowest hell for us, and from the womb of His finished work there issues the gift of eternal life as the gift of God's love to us.

The word "*upper*" comes from a root which means to ascend and to be high; and is often found in association with the act of offering the burnt-offering (see II. Sam. vi. 17, where David is said to have "*offered*" burnt offerings), because it was an ascending offering. Christ has ascended to the right hand of the Father on the ground of the offering up of Himself as a sweet savour unto God, and now the Spirit descends as Christ's gift to the believer. At once it will be apprehended that there is a difference between God's giving Christ to die on our account; and the gift of the Living Christ that we may live to God's account. Both are gifts, the

Christ is received by a definite act of faith; and the Spirit is received by obedience to Christ. It is not without meaning that Christ told His disciples to "*tarry* in Jerusalem." The Greek word "*meno*," rendered "*tarry*," and often translated "*abide*" (John xv. 4), gives us the secret of the Spirit's obtainment. To abide in Christ means to obey Him—"He that keepeth His commandments abideth in Him" (1. John iii. 24, R.V.). Christ is our Jerusalem, where we are to tarry, and as we do so, we experience that God gives the Holy Spirit to those who obey (Acts v. 32).

An Unmistakable Example.

The believer's eyes instinctively turn to Christ when he wishes to know any given thing or example, for He is God's revelation to us and the Example set before us. As we think of Him in relation to the Spirit we find there are two very distinctive experiences. He was born of the Spirit and baptized with the Spirit (Luke i. 35; Matt. iii. 16). The one was the commencement of His career as a man, and the other the initiative step to His call as the servant. There were thirty years between the two events. As to His humanity it is described as "that Holy Thing," or better, as the R.V., "That which is to be born shall be holy, the Son of God." With reference to His service the Spirit is seen coming upon Him as the gentle dove, and immediately after we have expressions which describe His utter abandonment to God, such as "full of the Holy Spirit," "led of the Spirit," "in the power of the Spirit," and "the Spirit of the Lord is upon me." The same twofold experience is associated with the child of God. The new nature

The Double of the Spiritual Life. 153

implanted by the Spirit is holy—"that which is born of the Spirit is spirit"—in distinction to the flesh, hence, believers are not seen in the old nature of the flesh, but in the new nature of the Spirit (Rom. viii. 9); and yet there is a distinctive experience as embodied in the expressions "full of the Spirit" and "filled with the Spirit." Believers are exhorted to the latter (Eph. v. 18). We are not left in any doubt as to what this fulness means. I can only indicate in the following points where the fulness of the Spirit is spoken of and the apparent results indicated.

Spiritual Worship. Elizabeth was "*filled* with the Holy Ghost," and blessed God in the devotion of her spirit (Luke i. 41).

Spiritual Testimony. Zacharias "was *filled* with the Holy Ghost, and prophesied" about the character of Christ's mission (Luke i. 67).

Spiritual Equipment. Christ was "*full* of the Holy Spirit," and was tested by the devil and overcame him (Luke iv. 1).

Spiritual Authority. The disciples were "all *filled* with the Holy Spirit," and were consequently under His absolute sway, for they spake as He "gave them utterance" (Acts ii. 4).

Spiritual Attitude. Peter was "*filled* with the Holy Ghost," and honoured Christ by his impartial testimony (Acts iv. 8).

Spiritual Courage. The disciples were "filled with the Holy Ghost," and declared "the Word of God with all boldness" (Acts iv. 31).

Spiritual Character. Stephen was "*full* of the Holy

Ghost," and was full of faith, grace, power, and joy in consequence (Acts vi. 5, 8, 15, R.V.).

Spiritual Faith. The first martyr of the Christian era was "*full* of the Holy Ghost," and was thus able to see beyond the seen (Acts vii. 55).

Spiritual Appreciation. Barnabas was "*full* of the Holy Spirit," and was thus able to appreciate God's work through others (Acts xi. 24).

Spiritual Discernment. Paul was "*filled* with the Holy Ghost," and was able to detect the devil's devices (Acts xiii. 9).

Spiritual Care. Being "*filled* with the Spirit," all life's relationships will be fulfilled, and their duties faithfully performed, as can be plainly seen by what follows the carrying out of the injunction to be filled in Eph. v. 18.

OLD TESTAMENT TYPES.

Three types we notice, namely, the oil and the meat offering, the oil at the cleansing of the leper, and at the consecration of the priests. *The oil and the meat offering*. Two things are said of the oil and the meat offering. Oil was to be "mingled" with the "fine flour," and the oil was also to be poured upon it (Lev. ii. 5), or "anointed," as in the case of the "wafers" (Lev. ii. 14). The fine flour is typical of the new nature which is the product of the Holy Spirit, the new life begotten by Him; and the oil is typical of His infilling and empowering presence. The word "*mingled*" means to mix with or temper, so that the oil becomes part of the thing with which it is mixed. The word is rendered "*tempered*" in Exod. xxix. 2, and "*mixed*" in Hosea vii. 8. The word "*pour*" means to "*pour out*," and by implication to melt or cast as metal, and extensively it signifies to grow hard, to stiffen, to place firmly. The word is rendered "*cast*" in 1. Kings vii. 24, "*firm*" in Job xli. 23, and "*stedfast*" in Job xi. 15. The word "*anointed*" means to rub with oil, and by implication to consecrate and to paint. It is rendered "*painted*" in Jer. xxii. 14, and is often used in the consecrative sense, as may be gathered from such expressions as "anoint it, to sanctify" (Exod. xxix. 36), "anointed Me to preach" (Isa. lxi. 1), "anointed him to sanctify" (Lev. viii. 12). Taking the three words, "*mingled,*" "*pour,*" and "*anointed*" in their typical application, they proclaim the truths of the Spirit coming to impregnate the life He has begotten, that He may form our characters in the firmness of His own holiness, and that thus we may be fitted for His service.

Cleansing of the Leper. The two things which are prominent in the cleansing of the leper are blood and oil. The blood is sprinkled upon him, and placed upon the different members of his body, and thus he is cleansed and sanctified (Lev. xiv. 7, 14). This is typical of the two things we find in the Epistle to the Hebrews, namely, the heart sprinkled from an evil conscience, and the entire being sanctified—set apart—by the blood of Christ (Heb. ix. 14; x. 22; xiii. 12, 20). In association with the leper's cleansing the priest took a log of oil, and placed some of it on the ear, thumb, and great toe of the man, careful mention being made that the oil is to be put "upon the blood," and then the rest of the oil in the priest's hand is to be upon him (Lev. xiv. 15-18).

Something very similar was done at the *consecration*

of Aaron and his sons. The blood and oil were put upon the different members of the body (Lev. viii. 23, 24, 30). The typical truths the blood and oil proclaim are, cleansing from sin and consecration to the Lord, and these are only possible upon the ground of Christ's satisfying atonement, and the Spirit's effective grace. The ear in its attentive obedience, the foot in its holy walk, and the hand of plodding service are the result of the Spirit's empowerment. Listening to what the Spirit says, walking as the Spirit bids, and working as the Spirit wills, we shall be designated, as was the priest of old, as the Lord's anointed.

THE SPIRITUAL WATER OF JOHN.

There are three references to water in John's Gospel, all of which are connected with the Spirit—"Born of water," "well of water," and "rivers of water."

"*Born of water*" (John iii. 5). That the water here mentioned is to be taken spiritually is beyond all question. Are we to understand it to mean as some say, "begotten of water, yes—and spiritual water, too," or are we to understand there is something in addition to "the Spirit"? I am inclined to think that John i. supplies us with the answer. John the Baptist came baptizing in water, and Christ was to baptize in the Spirit. Here we find the water and the Spirit together again. It is not without meaning that the water and the Spirit are together again at Jordan's banks when Christ was baptized. What was John's baptism? The baptism of John was symbolic of death and judgment. He baptized those who confessed their sins and plunged them beneath Jordan's waters as representing the death

The Double of the Spiritual Life.

and judgment they deserved. Christ had no sins to confess personally, but as representing us He went beneath the waters of death; and when He came out of the water, the Spirit of God, as ushering in the new creation, rested upon Him, as He had done on the chaotic creation at first. The being born of water and the Spirit seem to represent the believer's oneness with Christ as he dies for his sins in the death of Christ, and the life which comes by means of the Spirit as a consequence of that death.

"*Well of water*" (John iv. 14). Christ promised the woman of Samaria that the living water He would give her should be in her a springing well. This is no mere streamlet which may be dried up, but a well, or a "*fountain*," constant in its uprising (as the word is rendered elsewhere—Rev. vii. 17; xxi. 6). The word means a source of supply. The vitality of this water is indicated in the word "*springing*": it is rendered "*leaping*" in speaking of the wonderful evidence of the cure of the impotent man, who was not only seen to be "walking," but "*leaping*" as well (Acts iii. 8; see also Acts xiv. 10). When the Spirit is abiding in absolute possession in the heart there is a peace and joy which is beyond all description. There is nothing assumed or put on as the Spirit wells up, but there is a naturalness in the super-naturalness which is expressed in wholehearted obedience, quickness of response to the Lord, a ready willingness to do His work, and an alacrity and zeal to be and do as Paul expressed it, " to spend and to be spent "; that is, to spend all one has, and to spend out too.

"*Rivers of water*" (John vii. 37-39). The well

uprising speaks of the Spirit's leading in His upward work to the Lord; while the rivers flowing out proclaim His blessing from God to the benefit of others. Here again, no meagre supply is meant, but an abundance. The word "*rivers*" is rendered "*floods*" and "*flood*" (Matt. vii. 25, 27; Rev. xii. 15, 16). As water is life-giving in its flow, fructifying in its ministry, lifting in its power, cleansing in its use, and satisfying to the thirsty; so the Spirit in His operation in the yielded servant as He uses him in the service of the Gospel, is the Quickener of those who are dead in sins, the Begetter of fruit unto holiness, the Power to lift from the horrible pit of iniquity, the Cleanser of the sin-polluted, and the Satisfier of the soul-parched devotee of pleasure.

THE EXPERIENCE OF THE APOSTLES.

No one can ponder the lives of the apostles without seeing the difference in them before and after Pentecost. Suppose we take but one of the apostles, and look at some of the differences. Let us look at Peter:

Before Pentecost he was *self-authorized*, hence he said, "I go fishing" (John xxi. 3); after Pentecost he was God-energized, as we see and hear in the words, "Peter being filled with the Holy Ghost, said" (Acts iv. 8).

Before Pentecost Peter was *self-resourceful*, as is evidenced in his boastful "though all men forsake Thee" (Mark xiv. 29); but after Pentecost he is *God-dependent*, as we hear in his words to the lame man— "Silver and gold have I none, but such as I have give I thee" (Acts iii. 6).

Before Pentecost Peter was "*If*"-*burdened*, when he saw Christ walking on the water he said to Him, "If it be Thou, bid me come to Thee" (Matt. xiv. 28). After Pentecost he was *Scripture-certain*, hence he exclaims of the Spirit's visitation, "This is that which is spoken by the Prophet Joel" (Acts ii. 16).

Before Pentecost he was *self-acting*. He cut off the ear of the servant of the high priest (Luke xxii. 50). After Pentecost he was Christ actuated (Acts iv. 10).

Before Pentecost he was *cowardly* in denying his Lord in the presence of a maid (Luke xxii. 56, 57). After Pentecost he was *courageous* in the boldness of the Spirit (Acts iv. 13).

Before Pentecost he was *swearing* in his denial of Christ with oaths and curses (Matt. xxvi. 74). After Pentecost he was praising God with the rest of the disciples (Acts iv. 21-31).

Before Pentecost he was *trying to warm himself* at the world's fire (Luke xxii. 55). After Pentecost he had the *inner fire of the Spirit's baptism* (Acts ii. 14).

In the letters and memoir of Lady Maxwell there is a remarkable testimony as to a personal knowledge of the Holy Spirit. She says, "My former visitations from on high were either from God the Father alone, or from God the Son alone, or from both together; on this happy occasion they were from God the Father, God the Son, *and God the Holy Ghost*. . . . Hitherto I have been led to view the Holy Ghost chiefly as an Agent; now I behold Him distinctly as the third person of the Holy Trinity." Without discussing the mode of expression, there is beyond all question a distinct recognition of the Spirit to which Lady Maxwell refers, and which marks

Helps to the Spiritual Life.

an epoch in the life of the receiver; and whenever the Spirit is *thus* received, there is as much difference as there was in the lives of the apostles.

OLD TESTAMENT ILLUSTRATIONS.

I give a suggestive summary of seven of the Old Testament characters who had a definite second experience and spiritual crisis in their lives. Abraham responded to God's call to leave his own country, and although he halted at Haran, and went down to Egypt, yet on the whole he walked with God, but we find him listening to Sarah about the promised seed. There is a rebuke in God's command, "Walk before Me." He implied he had been walking before Sarah for thirteen years (see Gen. xvi. 16; and compare xvii. 1). When Abram got his name changed from Abram to Abraham, and he knew Jehovah as El-Shaddai, that is, God is enough, or the many-breasted God, thenceforward he lived in God's I will's of power (see seven I wills of Gen. xvii. 2-8), instead of Sarah's "I pray thee" of scheming (Gen. xvi. 2). God is enough for those who are Spirit-filled. They need no make-ups, or make-shifts.

Jacob was met at Bethel by the God of grace, and received many gracious promises (Gen. xxviii. 12-15), but he was afterwards met by Jehovah at Peniel, where God humbled him, and put his thigh out of joint. It was at Peniel and not at Bethel that he obtained "power with God and with men and prevailed" (Gen. xxxii. 28-31). The crushed and humbled spirit is the God-blessed and power-possessed one.

Joshua was called to be the leader of Israel in the

The Double of the Spiritual Life.

place of Moses, but there met him one day a greater than himself, Who supplanted him, and became Leader of the Lord's people (Josh. v. 13, 14). Joshua was anxious to know if the mysterious stranger was for or against him and Israel. The response must have startled Joshua, for He said, " Nay, but as Captain of the host of the Lord am I now come." Joshua immediately worships the new Leader, and obeys the directions which are given to him. The conquered saint is the conquering soldier. Those who have no authority of their own, but are under the authority of the Lord, have all the authority of the Lord at their back and disposal.

Gideon was in hiding and chiding till he got to the place of consecrated confiding. He knew what God had done in the past for His people, but he was burdened with ohs, whys, wheres, and wherewiths, till the Spirit clothed Himself with Gideon (Judg. vi. 34, R.V., marg.), then he goes forth trustful and triumphant, and Jehovah is to him a living, present, and a mighty reality, Who takes him through every difficulty and overcomes every obstacle. When we are only clothes to the Spirit, we are clothed with the Spirit. When God is in the dead past we complain and arraign, but when He is a Living Present we confess and conquer.

Job was one who had to be brought to the end of his good self. "The end of the Lord" that we are asked to consider (Jas. v. 11), is the way the Lord brought Job to an end. The Lord appreciated Job before He depleted him; but before He could give him the double He had to take from him the single. He had to bring his somethingness to nothingness, then out of the dust of his nothingness He brought into him His All-Somethingness. Man's displacement and effacement are the conditions for God's enthronement and enjoyment. The burning-up process was painful to Job, but it led him to the crisis of Job's ending and of God's entering, which was the secret of all his subsequent progress and blessing.

Isaiah's crisis came when he saw the Lord in His holiness. There was no doubt as to the negative side of Isaiah's holiness, but what he seemed to lack was the positive side of it. This is implied in his confession, "I am undone" (Isa. vi. 5). The word "*undone*" means to be dumb or silent. It is often rendered "*cut off*" (Hosea x. 7), "*brought to silence*" (Isa. xv. 1), "*destroyed*" (Hosea iv. 6), and "*cut down*" (Zeph. i. 11). The sight of God in His holiness made the prophet conscious that he was not in fellowship with that holiness, he was cut off from it, and silent in his non-responsiveness. He had been talking about the Lord in His holiness to others, but did not know the Lord in His holiness himself, hence his cry of the leper, "unclean." The Spirit-possessed man not only talks about the holiness of the Lord, but he knows the Lord in His holiness.

Elisha knew Elijah had something which he had not, hence in the tenacity of faith and devotion he clung to Elijah, determined to get the "double portion" (II. Kings ii. 9-15). He followed him from Gilgal to Bethel, from Bethal to Jericho, and from Jericho to Jordan, then after his master had left him he took up Elijah's mantle, and others knew the spirit of Elijah was resting upon him. The double portion of the Spirit's endowment is not easily obtained, that is, there are conditions to be fulfilled. The Gilgal of Calvary's

The Double of the Spiritual Life.

power over the Egypt life of sin must be ended (Josh. v. 9), the Bethel of the Lord's living presence needs to be recognized (Gen. xxviii. 19), the Jericho of the world's curse and contamination have to be left (Josh. vi. 26, R.V.; I. Kings xvi. 34, R.V.), and the Jordan of the judgment of God's sentence on the self in being crucified with Christ has to be experienced, then the Spirit as the mantle of God's power will rest upon us, and the difficulties will give way before us, and the salt things will be sweetened as was evidenced in the afterwards of Elisha's onward way (II. Kings ii. 14, 21).

Several other illustrations could be given. One other will suffice, namely, the experience of the children of Israel. Two distinct experiences are clearly seen, viz., the night of the passover, the coming out of Egypt and the crossing of the Red Sea; and the passage of the Jordan, and the entering into the land. These have their correspondence in the life of the believer. The passover, the coming out from Egypt, and the Red Sea experience of separation answer to conversion; and the passage of the Jordan of the death of self, and the entering into the land to the fulness of the Spirit. The wandering in the wilderness was no part of the purpose of the Lord, as may be plainly seen in the seven I wills of promise in Exod. vi. 6-8. The wilderness experience was the outcome of unbelief, which is another word for disobedience, and unbelief is the cause of all departure from God and the barrier to keep out of God's full endowment and equipment.

Hindrances to the Spiritual Life.

CONTENTS.

		PAGE.
	Introduction	167
Chapter 1.	Impurity of Heart	171
,, 2.	Worldliness	174
,, 3.	"Root of Bitterness"	182
,, 4.	Self	187
,, 5.	Failure to Make Restitution	192
,, 6.	Care	197
,, 7.	Cowardice	201
,, 8.	Evil Speaking	205
,, 9.	Pride	208
,, 10.	Prayerlessness	213
,, 11.	Neglect of God's Word	219
,, 12.	Unbelief	222

INTRODUCTION.

Tauler, the Christian "mystic" of the fourteenth century, says, "Why blame the sun for not shining into thy dwelling, when thou hast closed the window? Open the shutters, and then it will enter in all its glory, and spread warmth around. Thou complainest that the Lord gives thee nothing, that thou art not drawn of His grace, and dost not feel His nearness; only make room for Him, prepare a place for Him, open thy heart to Him, and enter in—the Lord is there: there shalt thou find Him."

The words of Tauler bring to my mind what a carpenter said, who, as he was enlarging a window, was accosted by the remark, "Ah! I see you are giving them more light." "No," was the reply; "I am not giving them more light; *I am giving them more window.*" The same thing is true with reference to the deep, full, glad, overcoming, and effective life of the Holy Spirit. The light of the Holy Spirit's power, holiness, love, and grace is flooding the whole circumference of our being; but too often it is not known, because there is failure to open the shutters to allow the blessedness of it to come in.

"Filled in* the Spirit" (Ephes. v. 18) is the Divine injunction. This command, in the manner of its interpretation, I am afraid, has misled some. The thought

---

* The Greek preposition "*en*" is more correctly "*in*" than "*with*," as the Revisers have noted in the margin of the Revised Version, and as Rotherham gives in his translation.

in it is not so much receiving a quantity of something into our being, as the jug is filled with water, but rather an entering into an atmosphere, in order that the atmosphere may enter into us. The way to get the ozone of the ocean into our lungs, that its toning influence may brace up the system, is to breathe it into the lungs, but in order to do this we must be in the ozoned air. How can we get the heat of the fire into the cold poker? The answer is simple enough. Put the poker into the fire, and then the fire will get into the poker. The same thing is true of the Spirit's grace; but in order that we may know Him in His grace, we must keep where He is found.

There are two main sources from which hindrances come to the spiritual life. One is from without and the other is from within. The former comes through the action of others, and the latter arises through something allowed or neglected. The Greek words " *scandolon*," and " *scandalizo* " which is derived from it, are translated " *stumbling-block* " (Rom. xi. 9), " *occasion to fall* " (Rom. xiv. 13), " *offence* " (Matt. xvi. 23), and " *offend* " (Matt. xviii. 6). The general meaning of these words is to ensnare, as when a bird is caught in a trap, to trip another up by placing something in his way, and to entice one on to his hurt.

Hindrances placed in our way by others. When others seek to keep us from carrying out the will of God they are a hindrance, as when Peter wanted Christ to keep back from the cross, which made his Lord say to him, " Thou art a *stumbling-block* unto Me " (Matt. xvi. 23). When fellow-believers indulge in things which they can take without any injury to themselves, but do not deny themselves of them, they may become a hindrance to us, for we, being weaker, and doing the same, stumble: thus they put an "*occasion to fall*" in our way (Rom. xiv. 13, 21; I. Cor. viii. 13). When others light the fire of unhappy division, they hinder and injure many by their unholy ignition, for their firebrands are "*occasions of stumbling*" (Rom. xvi. 17, R.V.). When others fail to keep in the holy realm of "the light" by not lovingly ministering to the brother in his need, then they trip him up by their unkind want of action, for, as the Word says, they become an "*occasion of stumbling*" to him (I. John ii. 10).

Hindrances which arise from ourselves. Christ says, "If thy right eye causeth thee to *stumble*, pluck it out" (Matt. v. 29, R.V.). "If thy right hand causeth thee to *stumble*, cut it off" (Matt. v. 30, R.V.). "If thy foot causeth thee to *stumble*, cut it off" (Mark ix. 45, R.V.). In these three passages of Scripture there are three members of the body mentioned: the organ of sight, the organ of labour, and the organ of motion. We may look upon things which may be hurtful to us, as when Lot looked toward Sodom (Gen. xiii. 10-13); we may do things which are harmful to us, as when David "took" Bathsheba, and had fellowship in sin with her (II. Sam. xi. 4); and we may go to places which lead us away from the Lord, as when Jehoshaphat "went" and "joined affinity" with Ahab (II. Chron. xviii. 1, 2).

There is one thing which will keep us right, and that is, to abide in Christ. "These things," He says, "I have spoken unto you, that ye should not be made to *stumble*" (John xvi. 1, R.V.). What things? If the fifteenth of John is pondered, it will be seen what "these things" are. Among them is the secret of fruit-bearing, namely, abiding in Christ. To abide in Him is to be obedient to His commands (1. John iii. 24, R.V.). Obedience is the sum and secret of the spiritual life. If we are right within through our obedience to Christ, there will not be much danger from things without, for the rightness within will give us spiritual vision to see the wrongness without.

There are many things which grieve the Holy Spirit, and keep us away from Him. Let us ponder some of these hindrances, which put us outside the Divine ozone of His holiness, and remove us from the pale of His power.

Hindrances to the Spiritual Life.

CHAPTER I.

IMPURITY OF HEART.

"Let us cleanse ourselves from all defilement of flesh and spirit, perfecting holiness in the fear of God" (II. Cor. vii. 1, R.V.).

God's Word has a good deal to say about heart purity, but we find some of God's children looking at the subject with suspicion when it is mentioned, because they imagine they smell that evil thing, "sinless perfection." Come, let us be honest. Do we not find some who hide behind the hedge called "Denial of sinless perfection," in order that they may have a little bit, only a little bit, it may be, of heart-impurity? Sinless perfection there never can be in this life, but Christian perfection there should be, and Christian perfection is the answering to God's will, even as the machinery answers to the moving power of the steam.

Impurity of heart may arise from various causes. Sometimes it comes through the open door of pure love, and leads down to the dark underground cellar of unlawful desire. Sometimes it will take its baneful brush, and depict, on the canvas of the imagination, scenes of unholy passion, like the ancients of Israel, who had filthy things in the imagery of their hearts (Ezek. viii. 6-12). The fire of impurity may be lighted by the torch of polluting books, which cause the mind to burn with hellish desire, and which leave behind them the smoke of remorse and the blackness of doubt. The sensitive-plate of the heart may photograph some scene upon it, through allowing the shutter of prayerlessness to be open; and the consequence is, an almost indelible impression is made which is never obliterated, although it may become dim. We may allow the barque of our being to be borne along the river of filthy conversation, and the slime of it clinging to us will be difficult to remove. The unholy touch of evil companionship will leave the mark of its black fingers upon us; and the evil beast of impurity will eat the flowers of grace in the heart, unless we keep the gate of the soul's garden locked by prayerful watching.

What is the remedy? Let the Lord Jesus, in the power of the Spirit, take the whole matter in hand. He will cause the David of true love to ignore the Ahithophel of unlawful desire (II. Sam. xvii. 23). He will overthrow the Dagon of evil imagination by the holy ark of His presence (I. Sam. v. 3, 4). He will burn the books of pollution in the circle of holy separation to Himself, as is illustrated in the saints at Ephesus (Acts xix. 19). He will exclude from the heart's temple the scenes of evil, even as Nehemiah cast out all the stuff of Tobiah, and chased an evil-doer from his presence (Neh. xiii. 8, 28). He will separate us from the mixed multitude of filthy conversation (Neh. xiii. 3). He will kill the Ahab of unholy companionship (I. Kings xxii. 34, 35), and throw down the Jezebel of impurity from the tower of our heart (II. Kings ix. 33).

Impurity closes the eyes to the vision of God, for it is only the pure in heart who see Him (Matt. v. 8). Impurity diverts the purpose of God, for the end of His commandment is love out of a pure heart (I. Tim. i. 5). Impurity paralyses the hand of faith, for the faith is to be held with a pure conscience (I. Tim. iii. 9). Impurity is the killer of true service, for the service of God must be done with a pure conscience (II. Tim. i. 3). Impurity is a stultifier of answered prayer, for those who are heard by God call upon Him out of a pure heart (II. Tim. ii. 22). Impurity takes away the appetite for spiritual things (Titus i. 15); and impurity is the companion of disobedience, for purity of any kind comes " in obeying the truth " (I. Pet. i. 22).

CHAPTER II.

WORLDLINESS.

"Love not the world, neither the things that are in the world. If any man love the world, the love of the Father is not in him" (1. John ii. 15).

As the trees by the lake side are mirrored in the water, so New Testament truth is seen in Old Testament incident. Where we may not take the incidents and characters of the Old Testament as actual types, we may use them as illustrations. The story of Athaliah thus illustrates the cause, the career, and the culmination of evil, and the curse which such persons bring on themselves and upon others by their conduct.

Athaliah was the daughter of the wicked King Ahab. Her mother was the idolatrous and cruel Jezebel. Athaliah married Jehoram, the son of Jehoshaphat. After the death of Jehoram, his son Ahaziah reigned in his stead for one year. Both father and son were influenced to an evil course of conduct by Athaliah (II. Chron. xxi. 6; xxii. 2, 3). When she found that Ahaziah, her son, was dead, she determined to destroy all the seed royal to gain the kingdom for herself (II. Kings xi. 1); but she was frustrated in her design, for Jehosheba hid the infant son of Ahaziah in the temple.* While Joash was growing up, Jehoiada, the

---

* Josephus says: "Coming to the palace, where Athaliah's executioners were murdering all the rest, Jehosheba found Joash, an infant of about a year old, amongst the dead bodies of the slain, which, it seems, had been concealed by the nurse."

Worldliness.

priest, in a secret manner, informed the priests and a number of soldiers of the presence of the infant king. Then, on a given occasion, Joash was proclaimed king. Athaliah, hearing the acclamations of the people, wondered what it all meant, and when she was told, she exclaimed, " Treason ! treason !" She was hurried from the precincts of the temple and slain. Thus ended the career of a cruel and wicked woman. She reaped what she sowed, and fell into the pit that she had dug for others.

There are many lessons which are suggested and illustrated in the brief sketch of this wicked woman. I direct special attention to one, namely, Athaliah's presence and power in Judah were the outcome of an unholy alliance. Many good men have made great mistakes, which have been fruitful of much evil. For example, when Jehoshaphat came to the throne of Judah, he " strengthened himself against Israel " (II. Chron. xvii. 1), but he made a threefold unholy alliance.

(1) When he " joined affinity " with Ahab (xviii. 1) in war against Ramoth Gilead (xviii. 3), and nearly lost his life (31). Association with the ungodly always means danger, damage, and distress to the servant of God. (2) Jehoshaphat joined himself with Ahaziah, the son of Ahab, in a commercial undertaking to make ships to send to Tarshish, but the ships were broken on their first voyage, and never reached their destination (II. Chron. xx. 35-37). Loss and damage again to Jehoshaphat; but he learnt a lesson, for he would not proceed in the unholy partnership (I. Kings xxii. 48, 49). (3) Jehoram, the son of Jehoshaphat, formed an alliance with the house of Ahab by marrying the daughter of

Ahab (II. Chron. xxi. 6), who is Athaliah (II. Chron. xxii. 2). Doubtless, through Jehoshaphat's intimacy with Ahab, she got to know Jehoram; hence the house of the wicked king of Israel became identified with that of Jehoshaphat. From this unequal yoke, Ahaziah was born, and reigned for one year in Judea after the death of his father. When Ahaziah died, Athaliah determined to kill all the seed royal, and reign over Judah herself. These are the links in the chain. Her wicked life is traceable to the blunder of Jehoshaphat. By forming an alliance with the house of Ahab he brought a blight upon himself and his house.

Do not parents—Chriatian parents—often make the same mistake when they endeavour to make "good matches" for their children? Alas! as some one has said, many of them turn out to be "lucifer matches." Better a humble cottage in the Lord than a palace in the world.

Worldly association always works mischief to the child of God. We cannot touch pitch without being defiled, and, being defiled, we shall defile others.

Worldliness is as *a parasite to rob us of the joy of the Lord*. As the ivy, by clinging around the oak, will suck away the life of the tree by living upon its sap, and will thus cause the branches to wither and die, and instead of the tree being a shelter and a pleasant sight, it becomes unsightly by its dead branches, so those, who, like Peter in the judgment hall, mix with the world, lose their joy in the Lord. Instead of witnessing for Him, they deny Him, and thus further the enemy's designs, instead of the purpose of the Lord.

Worldliness is as a *fog to hide the presence of the Lord.*

Worldliness.

As the sea-fret will obscure the harbour's entrance from the view of the mariner who is making for port, so will worldliness hide the face of the Lord from our gaze. Note, for example, the case of Abraham, who, all the while he was in Egypt, had no communication with or revelation from God.

Worldliness is a *damper to quench our zeal for the Lord*. As the stoker will damp down the factory fire when he does not wish it to burn brightly, so the worldly spirit will prevent our burning well in holy zeal, as the Judaizing spirit in the Church at Galatia hindered them from running well in the faith.

Worldliness is as a *leak in the hold, to spoil the peace of the Lord*. As a leak in a vessel will cause detriment to the cargo, so worldliness will damage the quiet of the soul. Lot found this out, when in Sodom " his righteous soul was vexed."

Worldliness is as a *tarnish to dim the Word of the Lord to us*. In reality, nothing can tarnish the pure gold of God's Word; but as a piece of silver becomes discoloured when unused, so will our appreciation of His truth become dull and lose its brightness, if, through worldliness, we neglect to study it prayerfully. It was so in the days of Eli, when there was no open vision in Israel, because of the worldliness of those who were priests in Israel.

Worldliness is as a *clog to hinder the power of the Lord*. As when the pipe through which the water passes becomes clogged, so worldly companionship will hinder the inflow and the outflow of the power of the Spirit of God. This is seen in the Church at Corinth, when they allowed one who was living in sin to leaven them with his wickedness.

Worldliness is as a *blight to mar the testimony of the Lord*. When a blight settles upon the fruit tree, it mars the blossom, and prevents it fructifying. In like manner, when a believer walks in the counsel of the ungodly, their company will act as a retarding influence to his fellowship with the Lord, as may be seen in the case of Solomon, whose strange wives estranged his heart from following the Lord.

The only remedy is to *live in the presence of the Lord*, to companion with Him and Him alone. When He is between us and the world, we are kept from its contaminating influence. When one is charged with electricity, but has no non-conducting substance between him and the earth, a great deal of the electric power is lost; but when a plate of glass is put between him and the earth, then the power is resident in him, because he is separated from the earth, and if one touches him, then the fire of the electricity comes out from him. In like manner, if we are in touch with those who are of the earth earthy, a great deal of our power is lost; but when Christ stands between us and the world, and the electric power of the Holy Spirit in His grace and godliness, in His love and liberty, in His truth and joy, is coursing through us, then there shall flash from us power and life, as men come in contact with us; yea, as they come in contact with us they shall come in contact with God.

Broadly speaking, worldliness is anything, or any one, put in the place of God. Conversion is turning to God from idols to serve the living God (1. Thess.

i. 9); and sanctification is separation to God from all that is contrary to His Word and will. Therefore, anything which makes us out of touch with the Lord is of the world, worldly.

Dean Lefroy, in enjoining a " self-denial week," in order to obtain money for a new organ, once said : " I ask that during this week total abstinence from every form of spirituous drink be observed. I ask that during the same period the enjoyment of tobacco in any and every form be surrendered. I ask that such amusements as are represented by concerts, by theatres, by the circus, be forsaken ; that luxuries in any and in every form be denied, and that the accumulated savings be, as an act of worship and a spiritual sacrifice, offered to the Almighty on the evening of next Sunday." The Dean sets forth a number of reasons why, for their own good, as well as for the work's sake, people should act upon his suggestion : " You will never regret the self-sacrifice to which I invite you ; you will enjoy the service of praise more which you have helped to enrich ; you will, probably, have made, in the period defined, some headway in self-discipline, and it will influence your habits, your home, and your character."

The appeal, we presume, was made to professing Christians, for no minister of Christ is warranted in appealing to the unconverted for help to carry on God's work. Presuming such to be the case, what right has a child of God to be mixing with worldly company, and living in luxury ?

There are two things suggested to my mind by the Dean's appeal, namely, a false premise, and a sad case.

The false premise is : To suppose a person to be a

child of God, and yet to allow him to mix up with the world. The teaching of the New Testament is: The believer in Christ recognises that Christ died to deliver him from the world (Gal. i. 4), that he is saved from it (Eph. ii. 5), that he is taken out of it (John xvii. 6), that he is crucified to it (Gal. vi. 14), that he is a light in it (Matt. v. 14), that the grace of God teaches him to abstain from it (Titus ii. 12), that he shows he has true religion by keeping himself unspotted from it (Jas. i. 27), that he contends against it (Eph. vi. 12), and that he obeys God by not loving it (1. John ii. 15-17). Therefore, the teaching of the Holy Spirit is, that those who belong to Christ are separated from the world; and to suggest that one may belong to the world and to Christ as well is to lay down a false premise and thus to deceive. The fact is, as the dragon-fly, when it leaves the pond where it lived in its grub state, forsakes the pond life for the clear atmosphere of heaven, so the believer in Christ leaves behind him the world of sinful pleasure, and is associated with the Lord Jesus henceforth.

The sad case is when any one, who has made a profession of faith in Christ, goes back to the world. Then it means one of two things: either he is a stony ground hearer, who allows the cares and pleasures of the world to choke the seed of God's Word (Mark iv. 19), like Demas (II. Tim. iv. 10); or else he is a backslider from the Lord. Like Abram, when he went down from Bethel to Egypt, the believer, when he backslides, leaves the tent of separation from the world, and the altar of fellowship with the Lord (Gen. xii. 7-20), and there is no joy, power, revelation, or fellowship, till there is a return to the Lord in humble confession.

What is the cure for worldliness? A firm grasp of the Lord Jesus Christ, for as we grasp Him in faith He grasps us in power (1. John v. 5).

Mendelssohn, on one occasion, hearing an organ being played, asked permission for a few minutes' play. The organist reminded him that he was a perfect stranger to him, and that strangers were not allowed to touch the valuable instrument. At last permission was granted, and then Mendelssohn brought such music from the organ as to make the organist weep. Ah! but before that music came forth there were two things necessary. The first was, the instrument had to be abandoned to Mendelssohn; and the second, he had to take control of it. The same is true with us. There must be the entire surrender to Christ first, and then He shall bring forth from us the sweet music of a holy walk, a lovely character, a loving disposition, a protecting peace, a sweet humility, a lowly service, a beautiful sympathy, and a Christlike life.

CHAPTER III.

"Root of Bitterness."

"Looking carefully lest there be any man that falleth short (Margin, 'falleth back from') of the grace of God; lest any root of bitterness springing up trouble you, and thereby the many be defiled" (Heb. xii. 15, R.V.).

The Holy Spirit says, "If the root be holy, so are the branches" (Rom. xi. 16). May we not say, "If the root be bitter, so is the whole nature," for as one drop of ink in a glass of clear water will discolour the whole of it, so a root of bitterness will embitter the whole being.

There are many things which may cause bitterness of soul, but they may be all classified under the following two points, namely, chafing under God's providential dealings, and thus being filled with complaining against Him; or else, through the unkind action of others, being fired with a spirit of retaliation against them.

When Naomi came back from her backsliding and wandering in the land of Moab, she said, "The Almighty hath dealt very bitterly with me" (Ruth i. 20), whereas if she had confessed the truth, she should have said, "I have dealt very bitterly with the Almighty." When a root of bitterness is rankling in the heart, it is sure to manifest itself in complaints against the Lord. The complaining all arises from looking at things through the coloured spectacles of unbelief. We put on the green glasses, and then say "everything is green"; whereas, things seem to have the hue we see, because we look at them by means of a medium we have adopted.

"I think if thou couldst know,
    O soul that will complain,
What lies concealed below
    Our burden and our pain:
How just our anguish brings
Nearer those longed-for things
    We seek for now in vain—
I think thou wouldst rejoice, and not complain.

"I think if thou couldst see,
    With thy dim mortal sight,
How meanings dark to thee
    Are shadows hiding light;
Truth's efforts crossed and vexed,
Life-purpose all perplexed—
    If thou couldst see them right,
I think that they would seem all clear, and wise and bright.

"And yet thou canst not know,
    And yet thou canst not see;
Wisdom and sight are slow
    In poor humanity,
If thou couldst *trust*, poor soul,
In Him Who rules the whole,
    Thou wouldst find peace and rest;
Wisdom and right are well, but trust is best."

From the human standpoint, the root of bitterness is generated by injury which is done to us by others, and it seeks to retaliate by giving to the injurer as bad as he gives, instead of following in the steps of the Lord Jesus, who, when He was injured, left His cause in the hands of His Father (1. Pet. ii. 23).

I well remember a brother in Christ saying to me one evening, when I put the question to him as to his being right with the Lord:

"There is one thing I cannot do: I cannot forgive my brother-in-law, who has done me a great injury."

"What has he done?" I asked.

"I don't care to tell you what it is, other than this—he has taken an advantage of me and done me a great injury, and I am bitter against him; in fact, I hate him. What is more, he is a professing Christian, which makes the matter worse."

"Do you know what the Lord says, when a brother offends you?"

"No. I wasn't aware He had said anything."

"Yes, He has. This is what He says: 'If thy brother shall trespass against thee, go and tell him his fault between thee and him alone.' Have you done this?"

"No, and I don't think it would be much use."

"You have nothing to do with results. As the Lord's child, He expects you to be obedient."

"But suppose he won't listen to me?"

"Well, the Lord then gives you a further instruction, and says: 'But if he will not hear thee, then take with thee one or two more, that in the mouth of two or three witnesses every word may be established.'"

"And suppose he won't listen to me when I have done this?"

"Then the Lord gives yet another direction, which is a final one. He says: 'If he shall neglect to hear them, tell it unto the Church: but if he neglect to hear the Church, let him be unto thee as an heathen man, and a publican' (Matt. xviii. 15-18). That is, he is to be treated as if he did not possess the grace of God."

"I am sure it will be no good."

"Again let me remind you, you have nothing whatever to do with consequences; what the Lord requires from you is obedience. Do you know what John Wesley did, when one of his companions in labour refused to apologise to him, when he should have done so?"

"No."

"Why, Wesley said, 'You won't apologise to me, then?' 'No.' 'Then I will apologise to you.' The result was, the one who should have apologised did so at once, being completely overcome by the kindly action of Wesley."

The brother did as I suggested, and the consequence was the difference was removed, and the root of bitterness killed; and more than this, he got such a blessing in his own soul, that he said he would gladly do the same again.

My reader, have you a root of bitterness in your heart—a grudge against some one? Remember, if you have, you cannot pray, "Forgive us our debts, *as* we forgive our debtors." Mark the "*as*." You pray that God may forgive you as you forgive others; and if you don't forgive others, how can God forgive you? Further, the command of the Holy Spirit is clear and emphatic: "Forgiving one another, even as God for Christ's sake hath forgiven you" (Eph. iv. 32). Mark the "*as*" again. Ah! This time it is not associated with a condition to be observed in order to obtain a blessing, but it is a blessing bestowed, which should be the incentive to make us act in a like manner.

Besides, this is Christlike; let us, therefore, pray in the words of one who is now at home with the Lord: "O Lamb of God, once slain! steep us in the spirit of Thy passion, show us the glory of Thy cross, let Thy mighty love melt our hardness, quell our pride, and so master us all, that each one may forgive his brother, though seventy times he has sinned against him. O Lord, our Vine, dwell in us richly, that so we may live with Thy life, and love with Thy love more and more, for ever and ever!"

CHAPTER IV.

SELF.

"He said to them all, If any man will come after Me, let him deny himself, and take up his cross daily, and follow Me" (Luke ix. 23).

Self is like a chameleon, it can take on many different hues. It generally expresses itself by affiliating with it another word to bring out its meaning. *Self-thought*, like the spider spinning its web from itself, evolves its opinion, and comes to its own conclusions apart from the Word of God, and asserts itself like Naaman did, when he went right counter to the direction of the Lord through the prophet with his "I thought" (II. Kings v. 11).

Self-seeking, like the cuckoo laying its eggs in another bird's nest, cares not what inconvenience others may have, so long as its own interests are served. As Lot, it ever looks out for some well-watered plain, although it may lead to the Sodom of iniquity and the fire of judgment (Gen. xiii. 10).

Self-confidence, like a bantam rooster strutting along on a dunghill, is ever inflated with its own importance, and elated with its own dignity. Like the Pharisee, it depends upon what it does, and is filled with self-gratification as it surveys the land of its own being (Luke xviii. 11).

Self-praise. Self-praise goes farther than self-confidence; it calls attention to its fancied merits, that others may admire and honour it. Like Diotrephes, it loves to have the pre-eminence, and like him, too, prates against those who oppose its arrogance with malicious words (III. John 9, 10).

Self-action. Where angels would fear to tread, self rushes madly in, like Aaron's sons, who, when maddened with strong drink, dared to bring strange fire into the holy place of the Lord's sanctuary (Lev. x. 1, 2).

Self-love. Self would move, if it could, heaven, earth, and hell to bring grist to its own mill. Its motto is, " I care not who sinks, so long as I can swim "; and, like Haman, it will do all in its power, regardless of others, to feed the evil of its own desire (Esth. iii. 8, 9 ; iv. 13, 14).

Self-will is the mother of all other forms of self, for when the regulator of the will is wrong, the time of the heart and life must be wrong too. King Saul illustrates this. He compromised the Lord's command by making it fit to his own will, and the consequence was, he damaged himself and lost his kingdom (I. Sam. xv. 12-26).

Now the first thing, in order to have a life all on fire with the love of the Holy Spirit, is to let Him fall upon us and press us with the withering power of His judgment, so that self may be blinded and unable to find its selfish way. This has always been the method of the Lord. Abraham must have every hindering earth-tie snapped, before he can enter the land (Gen. xi. 31 to xii. 1); Jacob must have the joint of his self-strength put out, before he can prevail with God (Gen. xxxii. 24-28); Israel must have the reproach of Egypt rolled from them, by the separating knife of circumcision, before they enter the land of promise (Josh. v. 8, 9); Achan must be judged, before Ai can be conquered (Josh. vii. 24 to viii. 28); Job must pray for his unkind and misrepresenting friends, before his captivity can be turned (Job xlii. 10); Isaiah must be brought to pronounce "woe" upon himself, before he can go forth on the Lord's business (Isa. vi. 5); and John the Apostle, on the Isle of Patmos, must be brought into the place of death, before he can be the messenger to the seven churches (Rev. i. 17-20).

"Ah !" says a believer, " I believe that self ought to be judged, and I know that it is only as it is in the place of death that blessing comes, but *my self is not dead, and it won't die*." A lady once said the same thing to Dr. Elder Cumming, and further remarked, " I don't find anything like this in my own experience. I have worried and fretted over the want of self's death. I have done everything I could to *kill* self, and it seems more active than ever !" The lady was making the same mistake as the unconverted make, when they want to feel saved before they believe on the Lord Jesus as their Saviour. What does the Holy Spirit say? He says self has been judged in Christ on the cross. His actual words are (I give Rotherham's translation of Romans vi. 6), " Of this taking note, that our old man was crucified together with Him, in order that the sinful body might be made powerless, that we should no longer be in servitude to sin . . . . so ye also be reckoning yourselves to be dead unto sin." " I have been trying to make these things true in my experience, and to realize them as my own," says a believer. Let me say that is where the mistake has been. Mark what the Holy Spirit says, " *Of this taking note.*" Make a note of the fact. What fact? That in Christ's death your sinful self is dead. "But," you say, "self is very much alive." Yes, but the Holy Spirit says, "Reckon yourself dead." What does the word "reckon" mean? The same word as translated "*reckon*" is rendered "accounting" in Hebrews xi. 19, in speaking of Abraham "*accounting* that God was able to raise him up, even from the dead," in calling attention to Abraham's faith, in his believing that God was able to raise up Isaac, even though he slew him. Thus we see to reckon anything is simply to believe God's Word for it.

How does the sensitive plate receive upon it the image of the scene before which it is placed? First of all, the camera is focused, then the plate carrier is affixed in the camera, and then the dark slide and the cap are removed; when this is done, then the light stamps upon the plate the scene before it. The plate is passive throughout. The light does the work. Something similar is true with reference to the subject before us. When the camera of God's truth is focused by the eye of faith upon the Cross of Calvary, then the Holy Spirit prints upon the heart of the believer the fact that he is crucified with Christ. It was not the plate which imprinted the scene upon it, but the light; so it is not the believer trying to make true in his experience what God says as to his crucifixion with Christ, but it is his allowing the Holy Spirit to make it true by an act and the life of faith. Now, when self would assert itself, faith remembers that self is dead, and says with Peter, as he said of the Lord, "I know not the man."

Too often believers get into the self-righteous Phariseism of self-denial, instead of following the Lord Jesus in the denial of self. What is the difference?

Self.

may be asked. In the one case you deny self certain things, and become proud of it; while in the other case the old self is denied, and Christ is followed.

Self is like our black shadow. When a light is behind us our shadow is thrown in our path, but when a light is in front of us, then the shadow is cast behind, and not seen. Thus it is with Christ and sinful self. When Christ is behind us, He but reveals the blackness and emptiness of self, and we are dismayed, and cry out, " Oh, wretched man that I am !" but when Christ is in front of us, and we are walking close to Him, self is forgotten, and we exclaim, " O lovely Saviour, Who can be compared to Thee; whom have I in heaven but Thee, and there is none on earth I desire beside Thee "

CHAPTER V.

Failure to Make Restitution.

"He shall make restitution" (Exod. xxii. 1, 5, 6, 12).

"If I have wrongfully exacted aught of any man, I restore fourfold" (Luke xix. 8, R.V.).

Sin is a trinity of evil, which cuts three ways. It lacerates the heart of God's love; it injures those who come under the influence of the sinner; and it severs the tendons of his own moral nature. There are three men who illustrate this threefold action of sin, each of whom said, "I have sinned"; namely, the prodigal, Judas, and King Saul (Luke xv. 18; Matt. xxvii. 4; I. Sam. xv. 24). The first sinned against his father's love; the second betrayed Christ into the hands of wicked men; and the third injured himself by losing the kingly position he occupied. The injury against God, He in His grace and mercy forgives; the sin against oneself may leave its stamp upon one, as the gash in the tree speaks of the instrument which has cut it; but the injury against another should be repaired, as far as possible, by the one who has inflicted it. Now when there is failure to repair an injury done to another, when the voice of the Spirit in the conscience distinctly directs it, then the ghost of the neglected duty haunts the disobedient, and the disobedience is a clog to hinder the wheels of the spiritual nature, and makes them to run slow, and even then, only at the expense of laboured effort, and lassitude of spirit.

Several illustrations have come under my own notice

where failure to make restitution has been a hindrance; but, as soon as restitution has been made, a flood of joy and peace has entered the being, like the bursting forth of spring after the coldness and darkness of winter. The following cases will illustrate: A young lad, in his unconverted days, in an evil moment of temptation, took two books, slipped them beneath his waistcoat, and walked out of the place of business. One of the first things which confronted him, when he was brought to Christ, was the stolen books. He could not restore them, so he wrote a letter to his former master, confessed his sin, and enclosed the money for them. The young Christian had the satisfaction of having done the right thing; and, further, he had borne his testimony to the saving grace of Christ, for he had told his former employer it was love to his Lord and Saviour made him do right to him.

Another case was that of a young girl who got out of a tram one day without paying the fare. The unvigilant conductor was partly to blame, but having listened to an address on restitution, she went to the tram office, stated the case, and paid three half-pence as an amount to cover her indebtedness. I need hardly say, after her act, the smile upon her face was like a May morning, bright and healthy; bright with gladsome joy, and healthy with a ruddiness which comes through being right with the Lord.

A young man, after an address on restitution, came to me, and said, "That address has touched me in a sore place."

"How is that?" I asked.

"Why," he replied, "I am a boat-builder by trade,

and some time ago I took some copper nails, which belonged to my master. I have never used them; they are at home, and I feel, after what you have said, I ought to return them; but I'm afraid to do so, as I may lose my situation."

"Consequences are with God. At all costs you must do the right thing." I prayed for the young fellow, especially asking that he might be true to the light given, and that he might find favour with his master. A few nights after, the young fellow came and told me he had confessed his wrong to his master, and that he had overlooked it. Then he exclaimed, "I'm glad those copper nails are off my conscience!" "Yes," I replied, "copper nails are apt to hurt, and they have pricked you."

I wondered why the young man still waited, for he made no attempt to go; but my wonderment was soon solved. "There is something else," he suddenly blurted out.

"Well, you had better have a clean sheet while you are about it. What is it?" I asked.

"Some years ago, when I was a lad in an office, I used to be sent by the clerk to get change. I discovered that he did not check it; the consequence was I began to appropriate some of the coppers each time I was sent for them. But one day the cashier examined the money and found there was a deficiency, and asked me for an explanation. Then I told a lie, and illustrated what you have so often said, 'One sin leads to another.' I told the cashier the money was given to me as I had brought it."

"Who was the cashier?"

"One of your deacons."

"How much did you take of the money?"

"About six shillings altogether."

"Well, you must repay it. Bring the money on Thursday evening, and I will ask Deacon —— to meet you."

On the Thursday evening we met. I asked the young man to explain the reason of our meeting. He tried to, but he could not get on very well, so I explained matters. When I had done, the deacon said, "I am quite content to let the matter rest."

As he was saying this, the young man pulled half a sovereign out of his pocket, and laid it on the table.

I replied, "No; you must take the money. There is ten shillings; give four shillings change."

"I don't want it," said the deacon.

"But," I said, "you must take it, even though you put it in the poor box afterwards."

The deacon was about to give the young fellow four shillings, when the latter said, "There is no change; for, besides the interest, the pastor told us in his address on Sunday evening the law directed a fifth to be added in all cases of restitution, as you will find if you look at Leviticus vi. 5. So, if you take the ten shillings, the whole matter will be squared up."

The look of grateful satisfaction on the face of the young Christian showed how thankful he was the restitution had been made; and, further, it told its own tale in the peace and joy which were evident possessors of his inner being.

My reader, are you conscious you have wronged any one, taken advantage of another's ignorance, failed to keep some vow which you made with the Lord, failed to render to Him His right in giving Him of the first-fruits of your substance? If so, confess your sin to Him, and to any one else who may be concerned; and then you shall find the light of God's love will brighten you, the gladness of His joy will bless you, the truth of His Word will cheer you, the holiness of His nature will bless you, the power of His Spirit will strengthen you, the consciousness of His presence will rejoice you, and the hope of His coming will inspire you.

CHAPTER VI.

CARE.

"Careful and troubled about many things" (Luke x. 41).
"Be careful for nothing" (Phil. iv. 6).
"Casting all your care upon Him" (1. Pet. v. 7).

"I have noticed a cloud on your face for some time past," said one friend to another, whom she knew had been worrying about certain things. The cloud on the face is caused by care in the heart, for when it is in the heart, it is sure to leave its stamp on the face, even as a disordered liver will colour the features. Shakespeare well says—

> "The incessant care and labour of the mind
> Hath wrought the mure that should confine it in
> So thin, that life looks through and will break out."

Incessant care had so wrought upon the mind of King Henry IV. that it had worn away his constitution, and made his life look through his being—so much so, it seemed that it would break through. Thus care ever frets the body, destroys peace of mind, and shortens life.

Care chokes the development of the inner life. In the parable of the sower, we are told the thorny ground hearers are they who are "choked with cares and riches and pleasures of this life, and bring no fruit to perfection" (Luke viii. 14). These words have an application to God's people. How often the work of grace is hindered, and the fruit of the Spirit fails to come to perfection, because of carking care, which comes and croaks out its wail, and lays its prolific eggs in the heart. The *cares of home life* will choke the grace of patience, and make the bitter thorns of distemper to hurt the spirit, and cause others to feel their prickliness as well. The *cares of business life* will choke the voice of prayer and the prayerful study of God's Word, and make the black thorns of covetousness and pride to grow with surprising rapidity. The *cares of social life* will choke the plant of holy separation to the Lord, and cause the sharp thorns of worldly ambition and worldly position to thrive to such a degree that children and Divine principles will be sacrificed on the altars of Moloch.

Care is disallowed by Christ; hence, if we allow it to come into our hearts and lives, we disobey Him. The command of Christ is, " Take no thought," or, as the word might be rendered, " Take no care." The same word as translated " *thought* " is given " *care* " in Philippians ii. 20. He says we are to take no care for our life, as to what we shall eat, and as to how we are to clothe ourselves (Matt. vi. 25-34); yea, he says we are to be " careful for nothing " (Phil. iv. 6). Anxiety as to temporal things is not to concern us, for the Lord promises, as we seek the kingdom of God and His righteousness, all these things shall be given.

Care is a robber, for the time we are occupied with it should be given to Christ. Christ had to rebuke Martha for being careful about many things (Luke x. 41). Martha was so full of care, that she had no time to sit at the Master's feet and listen to His word; yea, she tried to get Christ to censure Mary, because she was not so full of care as herself. Those who are blinded with care are sure to see faults in others. Thus Martha was a threefold sinner: she robbed Christ of her devotion, she blamed Mary for her seeming lack of service, and she cumbered herself with care. Christ desires the love of the heart before the labour of the hands; for He is sure to have the latter when He has the former, while He may get the latter and not the former.

> " Christ never asks of us such busy labour,
>   As leaves no time for resting at His feet;
> The waiting attitude of expectation
>   He ofttimes counts a service most complete.
>
> " He sometimes wants our ear—our rapt attention,
>   That He some sweetest secret may impart;
> 'Tis always in the time of deepest silence
>   That heart finds fellowship with heart.
>
> " And yet He does love service, where 'tis given
>   By grateful love that clothes itself in deed;
> But work that's done beneath the scourge of duty,
>   Be sure to such He gives but little heed.
>
> " Then seek to please Him, whatsoe'er He bids thee,
>   Whether to do—to suffer—to lie still;
> 'Twill matter little by what path He leads thee,
>   If in it all thou seek'st to do His will."

Care shuts the Lord out from the life. His Word of loving direction, with regard to that which would make life a burden, is: " Casting all your care upon Him, for He careth for you " (1. Pet. v. 7). Since He loves, and feels, and cares, it stands to reason that if He is shut out of the life, He is grieved.

CHAPTER VII.

COWARDICE.

" Ye shall not be afraid of the face of man " (Deut. i. 17).
" Be not afraid " (Deut. xx. 1 ; Josh. xi. 6 ; II. Kings i. 15; xix. 6; Neh. iv. 14; Isa. xxxvii. 6; xl. 9; Jer. i. 8; x. 5 Mark v. 36; vi. 50; Luke xii. 4; Acts xviii. 9; I. Pet. iii. 14).

One of the things which believers are commanded to add to their faith, that it may be supple and strong, is " virtue " (II. Pet. i. 5). The word " virtue " would be better rendered " courage." It signifies manliness, valour, pluck. Of the Crimean campaign it was said : " After all the discouragements and disasters, official mismanagement, army jealousies, camp sickness, and the discomforts of winter, the soldiers held on and took Sebastopol, not by science, but by pluck." A like spirit should fire the heart and life of the child of God—a holy determination to be right for right's sake, and a courageousness which keeps resolutely on, whatever the opposition is and the difficulties are. Now the antithesis to this is cowardice. It is a hindrance to the spiritual life, for it damps love, loosens energy, relaxes zeal, weakens faith, cripples testimony, stifles prayer, and grieves the Holy Spirit.

Cowardice damps love. Love will burn brightly on the altar of the heart if it is fed with the fuel of God's love, and fanned with the breeze of compassion for others ; but cowardice is like water—it damps down the flow of love's ardour, and discourages the warmth of Christ-like service to others. Cowardice was the cause of Peter's denial of his Lord; yea, so much had it chilled his heart, that he was afraid to own Him before a servant-maid.

Cowardice loosens energy. When the soul is bright with the Lord's blessing, then it is brisk about the Lord's business; but let cowardice put its hands to the sinews and nerves of the spiritual life, and at once there is relaxation, which leaves it devoid of moral force and spiritual power. Was it not so with Elijah, when he allowed a woman's threatenings to unloose his courage to such an extent that he desired the Lord to put " finis " to his life?

Cowardice relaxes zeal. When courage is enthroned in the heart, then zeal acts with promptitude and principle, as may be seen when Phinehas dared to do for God in the face of the camp of Israel (Num. xxv. 7, 8; Mal. ii. 4-6); but when cowardice is in the place of authority, then zeal slumbers and is inactive, like Jonah, asleep in the vessel, when he should have been telling out the Lord's message with fiery tongue and faithful ministry.

Cowardice weakens faith. Faith needs the support of the arm of courage. Faith, like the ivy which clings around and lives upon the tree, is dependent upon the other graces of the Spirit, and especially courage, for when this is lacking, faith is feeble and fainthearted. Bunyan well describes Mr. Feeble-Mind as being a nephew of Mr. Fearing, and makes him say: " He and I have been much of a temper; he was a little shorter than I, but we are very much of a complexion." Fearfulness and feeblemindedness both owe what they are to cowardice; for the former meets difficulties before he comes to them, and is made afraid; and the other is afraid to meet difficulties; hence, as Bunyan says, he had to be carried up Hill Difficulty.

Cowardice cripples testimony. The one thing which impressed the rulers regarding the testimony the early Christians gave to Christ was their boldness (Acts iv. 13). There was no hesitation in their utterance, nor trepidation in their manner; but in the power of the Spirit, and in the courage of their convictions, they bore their testimony to the Lord. But when cowardice has possession, then there is the very opposite; for, instead of the clear ring of certainty, there is the vacillation of doubt, which calls forth the remark from the unbeliever: " He does not believe what he says, or only half believes it."

Cowardice stifles prayer. Cowardice before men has its rise in want of confidence before God, and this again arises from a condemning heart (1. John iii. 20, 21). If we can look into the face of God with confidence, we shall surely be able to look into the face of men with courage. This was Elijah's secret when he was about to confront wicked Ahab, as he himself says: "The Lord of hosts . . . . before Whom I stand" (1. Kings xviii. 15). Christ could say: "The Lord God will help Me; therefore shall I not be confounded: therefore have I set My face like a flint, and I know that I shall not be ashamed" (Isa. l. 7). The same shall be true of us if we seek the Lord's aid in prayer; but let cowardice influence us, then the voice of prayer will be hushed, and courage lacking.

Cowardice grieves the Holy Spirit. The Lord is not ashamed to call us brethren. Why should we be ashamed to own Him as Lord? There is nothing which hurts Him so much as when we wound Him by denial, compromise Him by misrepresentation, and hinder His working by omitting to be faithful and courageous. The Holy Spirit is grieved when we fail to be true to His leadings, teachings, and commands.

Cowardice is disobedience. At the heading of this chapter there will be found some of the instances where God commanded His people not to be afraid. When He bids us to fear not and faint not, it is sin on our part not to be bold and brave. He who fears God need fear no one. He who can look God in the face with confidence (1. John iii. 21) need not fear to look men in the face with courage (Acts xxvi. 25-29). If those passages are pondered, it will be seen, the tasks may be difficult, the foes may be strong and many, men may be subtle, big words may be used against us, men may seek to discourage, the work may be great, the faces of God's enemies may be brazen, circumstances may be against us, death may be staring us in the face, and suffering lie in our path; still, in the face of all and above all, we hear the Lord saying, "Be not afraid."

Let us put away all cowardice, and at all costs be true to the Lord—true to His Word, by obeying it; true to His love, by loving each other; true to His grace, by being gracious; true to His power, by being strong in it; true to His purpose, by being conformed to Christ; true to the Holy Spirit, by allowing Him to bring forth in us the fruit of Himself; and true to His calling, by living in the power of the world to come.

CHAPTER VIII.

Evil Speaking.

"Putting away therefore .... evil speakings" (I. Pet. ii. 1, R.V.).

"Let all .... evil speaking be put away from you" (Eph. iv. 31).

A celebrated Persian writer says, "Having in my youth notions of severe piety, I used to rise in the night to watch and pray, and read the Koran. One night, as I was thus engaged, my father woke. 'Behold,' said I to him, 'thy other children are lost in irreligious slumber, while I alone wake to praise God.' 'Son of my soul,' he answered, 'it is better to sleep than to wake to remark the faults of thy brethren.'" The young fellow illustrates that those who speak evil of others have a good opinion of themselves. They take the supposed blacknesses of others as a dark background to bring out with greater prominence the fancied whitenesses of their own virtues.

Believers should not speak evil of others, because they are different from others. The "*therefore*" of I. Peter ii. 1 emphasizes this. Seeing we have purified ourselves, and that we are born into the Divine life (I. Pet. i. 22, 23), there ought to be a marked difference in our actions, especially in the tongue. Those who have the vulture nature of the old flesh we expect to feed on carrion, but those who have the dove nature of the Spirit should only feed upon the grain of truth. We cannot call evil "good," nor varnish wrong, and make it appear what it is not; but we can seek to remove the evil by rescuing those who are in its power. To speak about any evil we see in others is to show a want of love in our own hearts, for " love covereth a multitude of sins "; not covers them that the doer may go on in them, like a pickpocket who stands in front of his accomplice while he rifles the pocket of an unwary pedestrian, but covers them in order that the wrongdoer may have an opportunity to do better, like Joseph in his dealings with his brethren, who, while he was fully awake to the evil they had done to him, did not talk of it to Pharaoh and the Egyptians, but gave them a kindly introduction to his monarch (Gen. xlvii. 1, 2).

One who is guilty of evil speaking ignores the distinct command of the Lord, not to speak evil one of another (Jas. iv. 11); *yea, the command to " speak evil of no man "* (Titus iii. 2). A person was speaking unkindly of a third party to a missionary in the East, whereupon the latter asked, " Is she a Christian ?"

" Yes, I think she is," was the reply.

" Then," said the missionary, " since Jesus loves her in spite of all her faults, why is it you can't ?" The reply of the servant of Christ shows the way to kill the evil of evil speaking. If we look at others with the eyes of Christ, and see how He regards them, it will lead us to follow His example in regard to them.

To speak evil of others is to bring evil upon ourselves, or at least to keep blessing from us.

The late William Hake, of Barnstaple, relates how a Christian spoke evil to him of another. When she had done, he said to her, " What good have you done me by telling me this ?"

"No good."

"What glory have you brought to God?"

"None."

"What good have you done yourself?"

"No good."

"Then go and confess your sin to the Lord, and don't do it again."

For our own sakes, as well as for others' sake, and above all for the Lord's sake, let us endeavour to keep from us the evil of evil speaking, for it not only keeps blessing from us, but it proclaims evil in ourselves. Let us pray that the Lord will cleanse our hearts, and clear our vision; then we shall have a clean tongue.

> "Time was when I believed that wrong
>   In others to detect
> Was part of genius, and a gift
>   To cherish, not reject.

> "Now, better taught by Thee, O Lord,
>   This truth dawns on my mind:
> The best effect of heavenly light
>   Is earth's false eyes to blind."

CHAPTER IX.

PRIDE.

"The pride of life" (1. John ii. 16).
"Lifted up with pride" (1. Tim. iii. 6).
"Pride goeth before destruction" (Prov. xvi. 18).

Wordsworth says,—

> "What is pride? a whizzing rocket
> That would emulate a star."

"A whizzing rocket!" A suggestive simile. The sky-rocket whizzes up with a great fuss, there is a momentary glare, and an exclamatory, "Oh!" from some passerby, and then—what? The darkness is the more intense, and a stick falls to the ground! Pride is like the rocket: it calls attention to itself by its fizz, fuss, and whiz, and then its arrogance is the more noticeable by the ignobleness of its fall, and the contrast to the star of humility's grace, which shines on in the firmament of heaven's blue to God's glory, unconscious of its twinkling beauty and its beneficent light.

Some one has said there are four kinds of pride: pride of face, pride of race, pride of place, and pride of grace. The latter is the worst form of pride, for, as Hood remarks, it uses the saint's position for self's glory.

> "Shun pride, O Rae! whatever sort beside
> You take in lieu, shun spiritual pride!
> A pride there is of rank, a pride of birth,
> A pride of learning, and a pride of purse,
> A London pride—there be on earth
> A host of prides, some better and some worse;
> But of all prides, since Lucifer's attaint,
> The proudest swells a self-elected saint."

We shall be the better able to see the evil of pride if we see what it does, and seeing what it does we shall pray to avoid it, by God's grace.

Pride dissipates. Pride dissipates its opportunity to serve God, by endeavouring to get something to its own advantage. King Saul, as long as he was little in his own sight, kept in the path of obedience, but, elated with his own importance, he turned aside into Self-advantage Meadow, and dissipated his chance to serve the Lord (1. Sam. xv.) and so lost his kingdom. When the ambition of pride rides upon us, it will ride us to death if it can, and will stoop to anything in order to gain its end. A Christian lady in America was greatly interested in a Chinaman, who had made a profession of faith in Christ, but her hopes were shaken to the ground when, upon questioning him as to his motives in attending the means of grace, he replied, " Yi, yi ! me washee fol le whole conglogation." John Chinaman's idea was to get grist for his mill* in joining the Church; and pride does something similar when, in order to gain its lordly end, it allows the character to be dissipated by an unholy demeanour.

Pride aggravates. " By pride cometh only contention " (Prov. xiii. 10, R.V.). There is nothing so vexatious as pride. It cares not whom it puts out so long as it can get in itself. Pride is keen to detect pride in others, but the reason of it is, it wants that which makes the other proud, that it may be proud of it instead. " When Diogenes lifted his foot on Plato's

---

* For English readers, it is necessary to say that a great many Chinese in America are in the laundry business.

velvet cushion and shouted, 'Thus I trample on Plato's pride,' the Athenian sage justly replied, 'But with still greater pride.'"

Pride enervates. Pride takes the soul out of humility, the brightness out of joy, the life out of love, the fervour out of zeal, the love out of prayer, the grip out of faith, and the reality out of character. With truth has it been said, "He that is proud eats up himself; pride is his own glass, his own trumpet, his own chronicle; and whatever praises itself but in the deed, devours the deed in the praise." How true are the wise man's words, "A man's pride shall bring him low" (Prov. xxix. 23)—low, not only in relation to things in this life, but in relation to spiritual things, so that where there was humility and joy, there will be sickliness and sadness which accompany pride, as Hezekiah found (II. Chron. xxxii. 26).

Pride exaggerates. Pride puts a false estimate upon things, especially as to its own value, hence we read of the "*vain-glory* of life" (I. John ii. 16, R.V.), or, as the word "*pride*" might be rendered, "*boastings.*" (It is so rendered in Jas. iv. 16). An American religious paper relates the following story of rebuked vanity: "A certain Rev. Samuel Smith had been discoursing very learnedly and loftily, and was now walking home with his brother, eagerly waiting for some word of commendation. Not finding it forthcoming, he dropped a slender oblique hint, to see what could be drawn out. He was somewhat startled by the outburst, 'I tell you, Sam, what it is. Instead of preaching Jesus Christ and Him *crucified*, you seem to have been preaching Samuel Smith and him *dignified*.'" I am afraid the same might be said of many Christian workers. They make the Lord Jesus a pedestal upon which they can stand the statue of their own importance. Oh! the sin of it, that any should dare to make the Lord a stalking-horse for their own ends. Verily we must say of pride in such a connection as one said of hypocrisy, Pride " is the devil's stalking-horse, under an affectation of simplicity and religion."

Pride stimulates. Pride is like a stimulant, it makes the heart of conceit to beat with a false motion, hence it is said to puff up (1. Tim. iii. 6, R.V.). When the heart of the body is wrong, it often makes the flesh to swell. The same is true with the believer in Christ: if the disease of conceit gets into the believer's life it will affect the heart of devotion, and cause the body of his character to swell up with pride. And how sorry the after-effects are, as Shakespeare has well said,—

> " I have ventured,
> Like wanton boys that swim on bladders,
> This many summers in a sea of glory,
> But far beyond my depth : my high-blown pride
> At length broke under me, and now has left me,
> Weary and old with service, to the mercy
> Of a rude stream that must for ever hide me."

Pride overrates. Pride goes beyond the authority of God's Word. It prates much, but practises nothing. Like all who do not believe in "the doctrine according to godliness," it is " proud, knowing nothing, but doting about questions and strifes of words " (1. Tim. vi. 3, 4). Being "high-minded" (the same word as rendered "*proud*" in 1. Timothy vi. 4, is translated "*high-minded*" in II. Timothy iii. 4), it looks at everything to its own advantage, from its self-imposed position. Pride in overrating, generally over-reaches itself, and comes to the ground to its dismay, and very often to the destruction of its self-evolved plans. Let us beware of this thing, which is an abomination to God, and a woe to man.

Let us pray that we may be kept from this satanic sin of pride : from the *proud heart*, which lifts up itself against the Lord (Psa. ci. 5) ; from the *proud tongue*, which boasts of itself (Psa. xii. 3) ; from the *proud look*, which is brazen in its expression (Prov. vi. 17) ; and from the *proud foot*, which injures others (Psa. xxxvi. 11).

CHAPTER X.

PRAYERLESSNESS.

"As soon as Zion travailed, she brought forth her children" (Isa. lxvi. 8).

"Pray ye" (Matt. vi. 9; ix. 38; xxiv. 20; Luke xxii. 40; Acts viii. 24).

"Continue in prayer" (Col. iv. 2; Rom. xii. 12; Eph. vi. 18; 1. Thess. v. 17).

"What is it which has caused you to get out of touch with the Lord?" I asked a young Christian as she came to me, and lamented her coldness and darkness. "Do you know?" I queried again, as I got no reply. "Yes, I know what is the matter, I've neglected prayer." Too often the "matter" can be traced to prayerlessness. Loss of power in service, lack of fruit-bearing, leaving the first love, discouragement of heart, murmuring of spirit, unkindness of action, and wilfulness of way, all have their rise in prayerlessness.

We may often apprehend the evil of anything by observing its opposite of good. Let us therefore ponder the good of prayer, then we shall apprehend its evil by noticing its want.

In the Acts of the Apostles we have frequent reference to the power and privilege of prayer. Let us trace out some of its secrets as therein revealed.

Passiveness of prayer. Significantly it is stated, "they prayed," when the early Church wanted guidance as to the one who was to fill the place of Judas in the apostleship (Acts i. 24). They wanted the Lord's choice. Whether they were right in putting forward the two names for the Lord to choose from is not for us to say, but the spirit of their desire was right—they wanted the Lord's direction. True prayer ever desires to be on the plan of God's will. Prayerlessness goes on the opposite track: it acts independently of the Lord, like Abraham, when he left the Bethel of communion with the Lord, and went to the Egypt of the world (Gen. xii. 10).

Partnership of prayer. "These all continued with one accord in prayer" (Acts i. 14) is the comment of the Holy Spirit as to the persons previously mentioned. Prayer ever seeks the accord of united supplication, for it knows that the promise is to the "two" who "symphonize" together. The Greek word for "agree" in Matthew xviii. 19 is "*symphonize*," and suggests "a musical harmony, where chords are tuned to the same key, and struck by a master hand." As Dr. Pierson says, "Consider what a blessed symphony in prayer is to be found in the union of husband and wife in the Lord! May it not be to this the Spirit refers when He bids husband and wife dwell in unity, as 'heirs together of the grace of life,' and adds '*that your prayers be not hindered*'?" (1. Pet. iii. 7). Prayerlessness allows the hand of discord to put everything out of tune.

Power of prayer. "When they had prayed the place was shaken . . . . and they were all filled with the Holy Ghost," etc. (Acts iv. 31). Well may Tennyson say,—

"More things are wrought by prayer, than this world dreams of."

The power of prayer cannot be estimated, for when the

wire of our faith is connected with the electricity of God's power, it is then a question of His ability. Prayer has a *separating power*. The spiritual and natural sequence of Nehemiah's prayer was the cleansing out of God's temple (Neh. i. 5-11; xiii. 9). The same is true in the individual. Prayer has a *saving power*. The "Lord save me" (Matt. xiv. 30) of sinking Peter at once brought the saving power of the living Saviour. Prayer has a *solacing power*. Sorrow filled the hearts of John's disciples after their leader was beheaded, but they were soothed and comforted after they had "told Jesus" (Matt. xiv. 12). Prayer has a *strengthening power*. Heaven's angel strengthened Christ in the Garden of Gethsemane, after He had pleaded for His Father's direction. Prayer has a *spoiling power*. Jehoshaphat made his prayer to Jehovah when the Moabites and the Ammonites invaded him, and the consequence was, they were defeated, and he gathered much spoil from those who came to spoil him (II. Chron. xx. 6-12, 25). Prayer has a *staying power*. Paul would not have been the worker he was had he not been the constant pleader he was. The two references to "night and day" in his epistle to the Church at Thessalonica tell out the secret of his ministry. He was able to labour "night and day," because he was "night and day praying exceedingly" (I. Thess. ii. 9; iii. 10). Prayer has a *stirring power*. Let the Church begin to pray, "Awake, awake, put on strength. O arm of the Lord, awake," and the Lord will soon say, "Awake, awake, stand up . . . . Awake, awake, put on thy strength, O Zion" (Isa. li. 9, 17; lii. 1). Prayer always stirs us out of lethargy and laziness.

Let there be a lack of prayer, then there will be a want of power.

Perseverance of prayer. When Peter was imprisoned, the Church did not lose heart and cease to pray. Rather the occasion urged the saints to pray " without ceasing " (Acts xii. 5, 12). God's delays are not denials. He often holds out, that we may hold on. The importunity of prayer makes it intense. The word is, " Ask, seek, knock." There is not only to be the asking of request, but the seeking of repetition; yea, the knocking of persistency. " I will not let Thee go " is ever the plea and potency of prayer. But when the fire of the spiritual life is low, it shows there has been a lack of service on the part of prayer to feed it with the fuel of grace.

Preparation of prayer. " When they had fasted and prayed " (Acts xiii. 3). Mark the " *when*." There was no sending forth of Paul and Barnabas till they had tarried in the Lord's presence to know His will. We must wait in His presence to know His will before we start in His work. Elijah first laid the wood on the altar on Mount Carmel, then the sacrifice on the wood, before the fire descended (1. Kings xviii. 33-38). The disciples first tarried in prayer before they triumphed in power (Acts i. 14; iv. 31). What the grinding is to the sword, what the trimming is to the lamp, what the training is to the student, what the drill is to the soldier, what the pruning is to the vine, what the exercise is to the athlete, and what the refining is to the silver, prayer is to the service of God. Let prayer be wanting, and we shall fail to know the love and leading of the Lord.

Placidness of prayer. " Paul and Silas prayed "

(Acts xvi. 25). The apostles had smarting backs and manacled feet, but their spirits were free. In the cold of that inner dungeon they warmed themselves by prayer, and like a placid stream rolling calmly in some mountain gorge, they rested in the Lord, and heaven's peace filled their hearts. The flower of peace always blooms on the plant of prayer, for it lives in the soil of the Lord's presence. But let the rude hand of sin pluck up the plant of prayer, then the flower of peace is withered, and as it lies on the ground it is only a sad memento of the glory which is wanting.

Protection of prayer. " Prayed with them. . . . We kneeled down on the shore and prayed " (Acts xx. 36; xxi. 5). Paul felt that to environ the saints with the circle of his prayers was to set a hedge about them which would be a protection to them on every side. He was leaving the saints, and they felt it, as is evidenced in their weeping sore (Acts xx. 37), but perhaps their being left would cast them the more on the Lord.

There are many ways in which prayer protects us. Prayer is the *hand of weakness* which lays hold of the hand of God's power in the time of temptation. Prayer is the *cry of help*, which brings the Lord's aid in the hour of danger. Prayer is the *request of need*, which asks for the Lord's leading in the time of perplexity. Prayer is the *plea of sorrow*, which pleads for the Lord's grace in the night of distress. Prayer is the *pleading of endeavour*, which beseeches the Lord's enabling in the face of opposition. Prayer is the *voice of agony*, which cries for Heaven's strengthening in the Gethsemane of trial; and prayer is the *outgoing of faith*, which casts itself on the omnipotence of God in the need of daily requirement.

Neglect prayer, and you dam back Heaven's supply, shut out God's light, cut off the communication of His power, keep out the warmth of His love, the calm of His peace, the joy of His salvation, the vitality of His life, the vim of His grace, the comfort of His truth, and the cheer of His presence.

CHAPTER XI.

NEGLECT OF GOD'S WORD.

"Take heed what ye hear" (Mark iv. 24).
"Take heed how ye hear" (Luke viii. 18).
"A sure word of prophecy, whereunto ye do well that ye take heed" (II. Pet. i. 19).

The above three "take heeds" remind us that the only true word of grace, the only sure word of love, the only real word of wisdom, the only communicative word of life, the only certain word of assurance, and the only infallible word of guidance is the Word of God.

The late Dr. Andrew A. Bonar related the following incident: "A man once asked me, 'Is not conscience a safer guide than the Holy Spirit?' I just took out my watch and said, 'Is not my watch better than the sun?' Suppose that I said to you, 'I will tell you the hour by my watch, and you must always take the time from me.' That is conscience. It is the sun that is to rule the time. Conscience is fallen and corrupt. If we had an unfallen conscience, like innocent Adam, it would be as if my watch were always to agree with the sun. But now it is a most unsafe guide. Sometimes we hear men say, 'I don't see any harm in this practice; my conscience doesn't condemn it.' It is not your conscience or your consciousness that is the rule of right and wrong; the law is the standard. By the law is the knowledge of sin; sin is the transgression of the law, not of conscience."

The Word of God is the only true guide, for by it the Spirit leads. The words, "according to Thy Word," in the 119th Psalm, are illustrative of this. The cleansing of the life (verse 9), the quickening of the soul (verses 25, 107, 154), the salvation of the man (verse 41), the supplication of prayer (verse 58), the Lord's dealings in grace (verse 65), the kindness of God's comfort (verse 76), the utterances of His mouth (verse 91), the upholding of His power (verse 116), and the enlightening of His love (verse 169) are all "according to His Word."

We are exhorted as "new-born babes" to "long for the spiritual milk" (I. Pet. ii. 2, R.V.). What the food is to the infant, the Word of God is to the spiritual nature.

It is a well-known scientific fact in the animal kingdom that insects, and even the higher animals, become like the thing on which they feed; for instance, many caterpillars, feeding upon a certain vegetable, become so like it that they can scarcely be distinguished from the plant on which they are found.

The same thing is true with regard to the spiritual life. There is no more striking instance of this in the Old Testament than is found in the experience of Josiah. The direct effects of his reading the Word of God were the putting away of all idolatrous practices, and the earnest endeavour to perform all the words that were written in the Book of God (II. Kings xxiii. 3-25).

Correspondence to type is a phrase which is often used by scientific men to designate the likeness of one thing to another. The type to which we are to correspond is Christ, the Living Word, and this correspondence can only be obtained by the action of the Holy Spirit, as He makes true in our experience the principles which are found in the living tissues of the Word of His grace. Therefore, to neglect this Word is to be like the photographer who fails to pull out the shutter of the dark slide which contains the sensitive plate. The consequence is, when he goes to develop it there is no likeness upon it, for the plate must be exposed to the light to reproduce the scene before which the camera is placed.

Let us ponder the Word of God prayerfully, live it out carefully, practise it thoroughly, study it minutely, abide in it constantly, long for it ardently, use it manfully, believe it wholly, and mind it obediently, and then the life will be aglow with love, and labour for Christ will be a lightsome task.

CHAPTER XII.

UNBELIEF.

"Take heed, brethren, lest there be in any of you an evil heart of unbelief, in departing from the living God" (Heb. iii. 12).

"As far as I know, I have given up everything to the Lord," said a believer, who was distressed because she had not the joy and peace which she saw in others.

"Perhaps you have given up everything except your unbelief," was the reply of the servant of Christ to whom the remark was addressed.

We cannot be too severe in our strictures on the sin of unbelief. Its baneful and blighting influence is plainly seen, when we call to mind what the Holy Spirit has said regarding it, with reference to the unsaved. This is seen if the Greek word "*apitheo*" is pondered in the following passages of Holy Writ, where the word is rendered "*obey not*," "*disobedient*," "*believeth not*," and "*unbelief*." From these Scriptures it will be seen that unbelief shuts out from eternal life (John iii. 36), is the cause of persecution against God's people (Acts xiv. 2), is the mother of envy (Acts xvii. 5), hardens the heart (Acts xix. 9), is the forerunner of wrath (Rom. ii. 8; Heb. xi. 31), disregards God's entreaty (Rom. x. 21), is the reason of stumbling at God's Word (1. Pet. ii. 8), and is synonymous with disobedience (1. Pet. iii. 1). Thus the Christian should shun this sin as he would avoid a malarious district. We may further see the damage and desecration which unbelief accomplishes, in the following points, which are suggested by the setting in which the word "*apistia*" is found.

Unbelief hinders the Lord in His working. Christ could not accomplish much in His own town, and the reason is significantly given—"He did not many mighty works there, because of their unbelief" (Matt. xiii. 58). Unbelief hinders the operation of grace; it not only blights the soul of the sinner, but it binds the hands of the Saviour. Unbelief shuts out the light of God's beneficence, by shutting up the shutters of its own wilful way. It is a regular dog in the manger, for it will not have God's blessing itself, nor allow any one else to have it.

Unbelief shuts out from blessing. Of the vast host of Israel who were shut out of the Land of Promise, we read, "They could not enter in, because of unbelief" (Heb. iii. 19). Israel looked at things from man's standpoint, as unbelief always does, and everything was magnified in consequence; hence the sons of Anak and the walled cities were prodigious (Num. xiii. 28). The former could not be overcome, and the latter could not be scaled, nor brought down. Israel forgot how God levelled the walls of Jericho, and overthrew the Egyptians in the Red Sea. Unbelief is always troubled with a short memory. If Israel had viewed things from God's standpoint, they would have found, instead of being grasshoppers in the sight of the Anakims, the Anakims were but grasshoppers in His sight (Num. xiii. 33; Isa. xl. 22).

Unbelief keeps blessing back from others. The reason why the disciples could not cast the demon out of the afflicted young man was because of unbelief (Matt.

xvii. 20). From this we may gather that a want of faith on our part hinders the effective working of God through us. Again and again we read of the Lord blessing others for the faith's sake of those who came to Him on their behalf. The palsied man was healed for the faith's sake of the four men who brought him to Christ (Mark ii. 5); the centurion's servant was restored for the faith's sake of the centurion (Matt. viii. 10); the daughter of the Syrophenician woman was benefited for the faith's sake of the mother (Matt. xv. 28); the nobleman's son was cured for the faith's sake of his father (John iv. 50). Since faith brings blessing, the opposite is also true, namely, unbelief keeps it back. Faith is like Esther, it comes into the presence of the king, and secures blessing for its kin; but unbelief is like Haman, it brings devastation and distress to others, and woe upon itself.

Unbelief causes departure from God. The warning of the Holy Spirit is, " Take heed, brethren, lest there be in any of you an evil heart of unbelief, in departing from the living God " (Heb. iii. 12). There are many bitternesses which come through departure from God. The prodigal found the bitterness of dissatisfaction in his departure from the father's house (Luke xv. 13-20); Naomi found the bitterness of disappointment in leaving the promised land (Ruth i. 20); Abram found the bitterness of rebuke from the king of Egypt, in departing from the Bethel of communion with the Lord (Gen. xii. 8-20); Jehoshaphat found the bitterness of defeat through his unholy alliance with Ahab (II. Chron. xviii.); Saul found the bitterness of despair through departing from the commands of the Lord (I. Sam.

xxviii. 20); David found the bitterness of sorrow through his gratification of the flesh (Psa. li.); Israel found the bitterness of loss in being shut out of the land (Num. xxxii. 11). All these bitternesses have their rise in an evil heart of unbelief. We may well, therefore, shun such a hardening sin as unbelief, for it is the sin of sins. Man fell by believing the devil's lie, and he is saved by believing " as the truth is in Jesus." There is no more soul-elevating, sin-eradicating, and Saviour-exalting grace, than faith in God.

www.ingramcontent.com/pod-product-compliance
Lightning Source LLC
Chambersburg PA
CBHW060603230426
43670CB00011B/1954